For my June 1st guys, Van Cagle and Richard Dyer,
who were never far from my thoughts as I wrote

UNIVERSITY OF
BRADFORD

LIBRARY

This book should be returned not later than the last date stamped below.
The loan may be extended on request provided there is no waiting list.
FINES ARE CHARGED ON OVERDUE BOOKS

ALEXANDER DOTY

MAKING THINGS PERFECTLY QUEER

Interpreting Mass Culture

University of Minnesota Press
Minneapolis
London

Chapter 5, "The Sissy Boy, the Fat Ladies, and the Dykes: Queerness and/as Gender in Pee-wee's World," first apeared in *Camera Obscura*, no. 25-26 (Spring 1991), reprinted by permission of Indiana University Press. Gretchen Phillips, "The Queer Song," © 1991, lyrics reprinted by permission.

Published by the University of Minnesota Press
2037 University Avenue Southeast, Minneapolis, MN 55455-3092
Printed in the United States of America on acid-free paper

Library of Congress Cataloging-in-Publication Data

Doty, Alexander.
    Making things perfectly queer : interpreting mass culture /
Alexander Doty.
        p.   cm.
    Includes bibliographical references (p.   ) and index.
    ISBN 0-8166-2244-2 (HC : acid-free)
    ISBN 0-8166-2245-0 (PB : acid-free)
    1. Homosexuality in television.   2. Television programs—Social
aspects—United States.   3. United States—Popular culture—
History—20th century.   I. Title
PN1992.8.H64D68   1993
306.76'6—dc20   92-40036
                                                                 CIP

The University of Minnesota is an
equal-opportunity educator and employer.

Contents

Acknowledgments

There are many people to thank in connection with this book. First, I'd like to say, Corey Creekmur, you're a great pal and an insightful reader. When this thing finally comes out, we're going to put our feet up, have some champagne, and watch *Leave Her to Heaven* again.

This project took shape during the infamous mass culture year (1990-91) at Cornell's Society for the Humanities. Thank you, Constance Penley, Jane Feuer, Simon Frith, Rachel Bowlby, Laura Mulvey, Tim Murray, Mary Ahl, Aggie Sirrine, Linda Allen, and Jonathan Culler for the atmosphere of serious fun that prevailed during the year.

Cornell's first queer mass culture course members also contributed to this work in innumerable ways. I especially want to thank Colin Bailey, Heather Findlay, Jeff Schneider, Marc Arendt, and Alix Stanton for their intellectual and emotional comradeship.

Andrew Ross, Chris Straayer, Steven Cohan, and Constance Penley slogged through various drafts of this opus. It's nice to have good friends who offer encouragement even while they suggest you rewrite something just one more time.

Lehigh University's English Department remained steadfast in their support of this project, and of me. In particular, Rosemary Mundhenk, Elizabeth Fifer, Paul Winters, Vivien Steele, Carol Laub, and Ed Gallagher combined patience and wisdom when they were faced with occasional grand diva outbursts.

While they might not realize it, Biddie Martin, Bob Mundhenk, Chris Holmlund, and Michael Chesonis kept me going through their good-natured company and their interest.

At the University of Minnesota Press, Janaki Bakhle, Robert Mo-

simann, Gordon Thomas, and Ann Klefstad offered their enthusiasm
and helpful advice during those hectic months before production.

Finally, two special people endured long phone calls and face-to-
face conversations about everything-in-the-world while I was attempting to live my life and write a book at the same time: Jean Rosales, the
best Scorpio friend a Capricorn could have; and Bob Jacobs, the
Lorelei to my Dorothy.

Introduction

What Makes Queerness Most?

Taken together, the sections of this book suggest that the queerness of mass culture develops in three areas: (1) influences during the production of texts; (2) historically specific cultural readings and uses of texts by self-identified gays, lesbians, bisexuals, queers; and (3) adopting reception positions that can be considered "queer" in some way, regardless of a person's declared sexual and gender allegiances. Of course, floating around in culture is the text itself, which might be seen as a fourth distinct source of queerness. But unless the text is *about* queers, it seems to me the queerness of most mass culture texts is less an essential, waiting-to-be-discovered property than the result of acts of production or reception.[1] This does not mean the queerness one attributes to mass culture texts is any less real than the straightness others would claim for these same texts. As with the constructing of sexual identities, constructing the sexualities of texts results in some "real thing."

Having said this, however, I realize that at a number of points in the book I use language suggesting that the queerness I am discussing is incontrovertibly *in* the text, and that only heterocentrist/homophobic cultural training prevents everyone from acknowledging this queerness. Perhaps this is because part of my purpose in writing this book is to speed the process of removing mass culture queerness from the shadowy realm of connotation to which much of it has been relegated. Notorious for its ability to suggest things without saying them for certain, connotation has been the representational and interpretive closet of mass culture queerness for far too long. Since it has become what D. A. Miller calls the "dominating signifying practice of homophobia,"[2] the concept of connotation allows straight culture to use queerness for pleasure and profit in mass culture without admitting to it.

As with any concept of "the closet," however, while the regime of connotation (to adapt Miller) "has the advantage of constructing an essentially insubstantial [queerness], it has the corresponding inconvenience of tending to raise this ghost all over the place."[3] Given this, it often seemed that the most dramatic and effective way to overturn cultural and critical conventions that construct queerness as connotation was to argue that what had been (or could be) seen as "just reading (queerness) into things" was actually revealing what was there in the text. In conjunction with most of these statements about queerness-in-the-text, however, I raise and name various "ghosts" in mass culture production and reception that could lay claim to actually articulating the queerness "in" texts. As long as the analysis of mass culture remains dependent primarily upon texts, with their unstable representational codes, as the alpha and the omega of proof of queerness, the queerness of and in mass culture will remain "essentially insubstantial," as it will remain in the twilight zone of connotation.

"Uncloseted" or brought forward by equal attention to producers and readers, however, the queerness in and of mass culture might be used to challenge the politics of denotation and connotation as it is traditionally deployed in discussing texts and representation. In this way the closet of connotation could be dismantled, rejected for the oppressive practice it is. After all, the queerness I point out in mass culture representation and reading in this book is only "connotative," and therefore deniable or "insubstantial" as long as we keep thinking within conventional heterocentrist paradigms, which always already have decided that expressions of queerness are *sub*-textual, *sub*-cultural, *alternative* readings, or pathetic and delusional attempts to see something that isn't there—after all, mass culture texts are made for the "average" (straight, white, middle-class, usually male) person, aren't they? I've got news for straight culture: your readings of texts are usually "alternative" ones for me, and they often seem like desperate attempts to deny the queerness that is so clearly a part of mass culture. The day someone can establish without a doubt that images and other representations of men and women getting married, with their children, or even having sex, undeniably depict "straightness," is the day someone can say no lesbian or gay has ever been married, had children from heterosexual intercourse, or had sex with someone of the other gender for any reason.

In analyzing mass culture queerness, I often found myself within complicated discursive spaces when I considered how cultural heterocentrism and homophobia of the kind suggested above influences our understanding of the text/representation, as well as our understanding of the producers and readers of mass culture. As a result, my discussions of reception, authorship, narrative, genres, and star images attempt both to describe how and where certain heterocentrist critical and theoretical approaches to mass culture work, and to suggest how and where the queerness of texts, producers, and readers might be discussed outside these heterocentrist and homophobic discursive frames.

I find Michael Warner's discussion of queer theory's great investment in the text interesting in this context, as it implies that the queerness of texts is pervasive and yet not obvious to heterocentrist straights:

> Almost everything that would be called queer theory is about ways in which texts—either literature or mass culture or language—shape sexuality. Usually, the notion is that fantasy and other kinds of representation are inherently uncontrollable, queer by nature. This focus on messy representation allows queer theory, like non-academic queer activism, to be both antiassimilationist and antiseparatist: you can't eliminate queerness, says queer theory, or screen it out. It's everywhere. There's no place to hide, hetero scum![4]

While he initially focuses upon the text and representation in his summary of "what makes queer theory most," Warner quickly branches out to suggest that fantasy and politics are equally important in discussing queerness. Unable to accurately describe queer theory only in terms of textual fetishism, Warner's comments here are a good example of how difficult it can be to attribute the queerness of mass culture to just one source or another. Then there are those moments of "multiple queerness," when a number of distinct, sometimes contradictory, queer aspects or approaches suggest themselves in the face of a mass culture event.

So while I try to be as clear and coherent as possible about discussing the sources of queerness in the material that follows, the complexity and volatility of mass culture production and reception-consumption often make any attempt to attribute queerness to only (or mostly) producers, texts, or audiences seem false and limiting. For example, chapter 3 analyzes narrative construction in order to establish its central argument—that sitcoms such as *Laverne and Shirley* might be called "lesbian." Yet the discussions of audience pleasure and character development that are connected to the textual analyses here gradually move away from the text as the source of queerness to find other sites of queerness in reception and within specific lesbian cultural coding and reading practices. This section also suggests that the various types of queerness "in" these sitcoms can be understood with reference to a number of political agendas.

But this critical-theoretical-political "messiness" about coming to a bottom line about queerness and "what makes queerness most" is actually one of the strengths in this early period of queer identity, culture, and theory formation. Teresa de Lauretis's comments about recent work to "reconceptualize . . . homosexualities" could apply to current attempts to establish queerness as an identity, a politics, and a theory, as queer discourse often seems "fuzzily defined, undercoded, or discursively dependent on more established forms."[5] If at the moment no particular definition or use of "queer" and "queerness" has gained wide currency, however, there have been a number of interesting and influential definitional propositions.

Queer Nation's use of the term most often sets up queerness as something different from gay, lesbian, and bisexual assimilationism. In this case, to identify as a queer means to be politically radical and "in-your-face": to paradoxically demand recognition by straight culture while at the same time rejecting this culture.[6] Part of what is being rejected here are attempts to contain people through labeling, so "queer" is touted as an inclusive, but not exclusive, category, unlike "straight," "gay," "lesbian," or "bisexual." But many commentators have pointed out the contradictions between Queer Nation's specific political stance and its claims that "queer," as they use it, is an inclusive category. Miguel Gutierrez, for one, sees race and class issues limiting the inclusiveness of Queer Nation's queerness: "There are people who cannot afford to be nonassimilationist; they are fighting just to eat and live."[7]

Among academic theorists, Teresa de Lauretis, in a note to her introduction for the "Queer Theory" issue of *differences*, says that her "queer" has "no relation to the Queer Nation group." What de Lauretis's "queer" does appear to represent is a way of rethinking gay and lesbian identities and cultures

> based on the speculative premise that homosexuality is no longer to be seen simply as marginal with regard to a dominant, stable form of sexuality (heterosexuality) against which it would be defined either by

opposition or by homology. In other words, it is no longer to be seen either as merely transgressive or deviant vis-à-vis a proper, natural sexuality . . . according to the older pathological model, or as just another, optional "life-style," according to the model of contemporary North American pluralism. . . . Thus, rather than marking the limits of the social space by designating a place at the edge of culture, gay sexuality in its specific female and male cultural (or subcultural) forms acts as an agency of social process whose mode of functioning is both interactive and yet resistant, both participatory and yet distinct, claiming at once equality and difference.[8]

Where de Lauretis retains the categories "gay" and "lesbian" and some notion of gender division as parts of her discussion of what "queerness" is (or might be), Judith Butler and Sue-Ellen Case have argued that queerness is something that is ultimately beyond gender—it is an attitude, a way of responding, that begins in a place not concerned with, or limited by, notions of a binary opposition of male and female or the homo versus hetero paradigm usually articulated as an extention of this gender binarism.[9]

Since working with(in) queerness is only a few years old in activism and in academe, however, this seems more a time for questions and proposals than hard-and-fast defining statements. After all, in any of its uses so far, queerness has been set up to challenge and break apart conventional categories, not to become one itself. De Lauretis precisely describes the elusive quality of queerness I want to suggest in my readings of mass culture when she describes it as "both interactive yet resistant, both participatory yet distinct."[10] And while the notion of queer and queerness I use in this book borrows Queer Nation's goal of inclusivity, it does not limit queer expression to a certain political agenda. Any "queerer than thou" attitude, based on politics, style, sexual behavior, or any other quality, can only make queerness become something other than an open and flexible space. Queerness, in the way this book uses it, is a quality related to any expression that can be marked as contra-, non-, or anti-straight. So, as far as cultural production and reception are concerned, a conservative gay white male's response to Mel Gibson's star image is as queer as one of Sadie Benning's punkish "baby-dyke" videos.

While this brand of queerness may seem blandly democratic, I ultimately use it to question the cultural demarcations between the queer and the straight (made by both queers and straights) by pointing out the queerness of and in straights and straight cultures, as well as that of individuals and groups who have been told they inhabit the boundaries between the binaries of gender and sexuality: transsexuals, bisexuals, transvestites, and other binary outlaws. Therefore, when I use the terms "queer" or "queerness" as adjectives or nouns, I do so to suggest a range of nonstraight expression in, or in response to, mass culture. This range includes specifically gay, lesbian, and bisexual expressions; but it also includes all other potential (and potentially unclassifiable) nonstraight positions.

This being the case, I like those uses of "queer" that make it more than just an umbrella term in the ways that "homosexual" and "gay" have been used to mean lesbian *or* gay *or* bisexual, because queerness can also be about the intersecting or combining of more than one specific form of nonstraight sexuality. For example, when a text such as *Gentlemen Prefer Blondes* accumulates lesbian, gay, and bisexual responses, sometimes in relation to the same spectator, we have a queer text and queer reader, rather than a specifically lesbian or gay or bisexual text and reader. Queer would also describe the image of Katharine Hepburn dressed as a young man in *Sylvia Scarlett*, as it evokes complex, often uncategorizable, erotic responses from spectators who claim all sorts of real-life sexual identities.

But whereas I would call certain straight and gay male pleasures in *The Mary Tyler Moore Show* "queer," I would still use the term "lesbian" to describe the text's basic narrative construction and the pleasures dykes might take in the show. In working out ideas about queerness in mass culture, I often found it necessary to discuss the queerness of mass culture texts, producers, and readers with reference to particular nonstraight positions. This being the case, rhetorical shifts between queer/queerness and lesbian/lesbianism (or gay/gayness, bisexual/bisexuality) in this book are less signs of contradiction than they are attempts to mediate between the impulse to deconstruct established sexual and gender categories and the feeling that these categories need to be considered because they represent important cultural and political positions.

Working out a rhetorical strategy that clearly and consistently mediates between using established sexual identity labels and using "queer" has been difficult, however, particularly where I discuss texts and reader responses simultaneously. To refer to the example above, is it accurate to say that only self-identified dykes can have "lesbian" pleasures in the lesbian narrative of a program like *The Mary Tyler Moore Show*? If so, then would "queer" be used to describe the responses of nonlesbians to the show, so that gay men could be said to take queer pleasures in the lesbian narratives of *The Mary*

Tyler Moore Show? But couldn't nonlesbians be taking specifically *lesbian* pleasures in the program's narratives? Might we go on to say that *The Mary Tyler Moore Show*'s narratives encourage a specifically lesbian positioning vis-à-vis the text for *all* viewers?

Considering my definition and uses of "queer," I could find no easy solution to this rhetorical dilemma, as questions like the ones above are related to questions of labeling, essentialism, and sexual identity, as well to the political uses of these ideas. At this point, I find myself working with sexual identity terms in the service of not-quite-compatible goals. I want to construct "queer" as something other than "lesbian," "gay," or "bisexual"; but I can't say that "lesbian," "gay," or "bisexual" *aren't* also "queer." I would like to maintain the integrity of "lesbian," "gay," and "bisexual" as concepts that have specific historical, cultural, and personal meanings; but I would also like "lesbian," "gay," and "bisexual" culture, history, theory, and politics to have some bearing on the articulation of queerness. On the other hand, it seems important not to have "queer" and "queerness" become the type of umbrella terms that implicitly position "lesbian," "gay," and "bisexual" erotics, cultures, and politics as mere subsets of some larger, and seemingly more complex, progressive, or politically efficacious concept. This has already happened to lesbians in relation to notions of "women," "feminism," "homosexuality," and "gayness."

Alisa Solomon's questions—"Can queer politics be forged *without* a gay or lesbian identity? And what would that be like?"—reflect a historical period during which many of us feel the need to continue referring to those established sexual and gender categories we've lived and worked under for so long, while simultaneously attempting to understand, and to articulate, the ways in which these categories don't quite represent our attitudes.[11] "It is the queer in me that empowers," says Carol A. Queen, "—that lets me see those lines and burn to cross them."[12] This book was written from within this type of transitional cultural and theoretical space, as it recognizes gender and sexual "lines" while suggesting ways to question our understanding of how those lines function in mass culture production and reception. Ultimately, queerness should challenge and confuse our understanding and uses of sexual and gender categories. In order to maintain some level of coherence and consistency in my use of sexual identity labels in this work, however, I have effected certain rhetorical compromises. While I never expected these compromises to answer every sticky theoretical or political question surrounding my uses of "queer," "lesbian," "gay," and "bisexual" in relation to mass culture, at least these rhetorical decisions allowed me to consider these questions with some degree of complexity.

I decided to employ "lesbian," "gay," and "bisexual" when discussing texts or textual elements that work within monogender or nonstraight bigender dynamics (such as the lesbian sitcom narrative structure of *Laverne and Shirley*). "Queer" texts/textual elements, then, are those discussed with reference to a range or a network of nonstraight ideas. The queerness in these cases might combine the lesbian, the gay, and the bisexual, or it might be a textual queerness not accurately described even by a combination of these labels—such as the range of queerness in *Sylvia Scarlett*. As far as mass culture producers and reader-consumers are concerned, "lesbian," "gay," and "bisexual" are reserved in this book to describe the work, positions, pleasures, and readings of self-identified lesbians, gays, and bisexuals as they relate to sexually parallel areas in textual production or reception. So, I would call a gay's erotic response to the central male pair in *Rope* "gay," but I would not use "gay" to describe this same person's erotic response to the lesbian porn film *Clips*. This I would call "queer" (or perhaps even "straight," depending on the nature of the response). Therefore, "queer" is used to describe the nonstraight work, positions, pleasures, and readings of people who either don't share the same "sexual orientation" as that articulated in the texts they are producing or responding to (the gay man who takes queer pleasure in a lesbian sitcom narrative, for example), or who don't define themselves as lesbian, gay, bisexual (or straight, for that matter). Finally, "queer" is occasionally used as an umbrella term, à la "homosexual," when I want to make a collective point about lesbians, and/or gays, and/or bisexuals, and/or queers (whether self-identified queers or queer-positioned nonqueers).

Given all of this, the queerness of and in this book is not something that is always distinctly different from "just" gayness, or lesbianism, or bisexuality—although it can be, as in cases of straight queerness, and of other forms of queerness that might not be contained within existing categories or have reference to only one established category. If this approach isn't always rigorous and precise about defining and theorizing separate "new" areas in mass culture production, reception, and textual analysis that are nonstraight as well as nonlesbian/nongay/nonbisexual, I would hope the book's inclusive approach finally suggests that new queer spaces open up (or are revealed) whenever someone moves away from using only one specific sexual identity category — gay, lesbian, bisexual, or straight — to understand and to describe mass culture, and recognizes that texts and people's responses to them are more sexually transmutable than any one category could signify — excepting, perhaps, that of "queer."[13]

CHAPTER ONE

There's Something Queer Here

But standing before the work of art requires you to act too.
The tension you bring to the work of art is an action.

Jean Genet[1]

I'm gonna take you to queer bars
I'm gonna drive you in queer cars
You're gonna meet all of my queer friends
Our queer, queer fun it never ends.

"The Queer Song,"
Gretchen Phillips, Two Nice Girls[2]

The most slippery and elusive terrain for mass culture studies continues to be negotiated within audience and reception theory. Perhaps this is because within cultural studies, "audience" is now always already acknowledged to be fragmented, polymorphous, contradictory, and "nomadic," whether in the form of individual or group subjects. Given this, it seems an almost impossible task to conduct reception studies that capture the complexity of those moments in which audiences meet mass culture texts. As Janice Radway puts it:

> No wonder we find it so difficult to theorize the dispersed, anonymous, unpredictable nature of the use of mass-produced, mass-mediated cultural forms. If the receivers of such forms are never assembled fixedly on a site or even in an easily identifiable space, if they are frequently not uniformly or even attentively disposed to systems of cultural production or to the messages they issue, how can we theorize, not to mention examine, the ever-shifting kaleidoscope of cultural circulation and consumption?[3]

In confronting this complexity, Radway suggests that mass culture

1

studies begin to analyze reception more ethnographically by focusing upon the dense patterns and practices "of daily life and the way in which the media are integrated and implicated within it," rather than starting with already established audience categories.[4] Clearly the danger of making essentializing statements about both audiences and their reception practices lurks behind any uncritical use of categories such as "women," "teenagers," "lesbians," "housewives," "blue-collar workers," "blacks," or "gay men." Further, conducting reception studies on the basis of conventional audience categories can also lead to critical blindness about how certain reception strategies are shared by otherwise disparate individuals and groups.

I would like to propose "queerness" as a mass culture reception practice that is shared by all sorts of people in varying degrees of consistency and intensity.[5] Before proceeding, however, I will need to discuss—even defend—my use of "queer" in such phrases as "queer positions," "queer readers," "queer readings," and "queer discourses." In working through my thoughts on gay and lesbian cultural history, I found that while I used "gay" to describe particulars of men's culture, and "lesbian" to describe particulars of women's culture, I was hard-pressed to find a term to describe a cultural common ground between lesbians and gays as well as other nonstraights—a term representing unity as well as suggesting diversity. For certain historical and political reasons, "queer" suggested itself as such a term. As Adele Morrison said in an OUT/LOOK interview: "Queer is not an 'instead of,' it's an 'inclusive of.' I'd never want to lose the terms that specifically identify me."[6]

Currently, the word "gay" doesn't consistently have the same gender-unifying quality it may once have possessed. And since I'm interested in discussing aspects of cultural identification as well as of sexual desire, "homosexual" will not do either. I agree with those who do not find the word "homosexual" an appropriate synonym for both "gay" and "lesbian," as these latter terms are constructions that concern more than who you sleep with—although the objects of sexual desires are certainly central to expressions of lesbian and gay cultural identities. I also wanted to find a term with some ambiguity, a term that would describe a wide range of impulses and cultural expressions, including space for describing and expressing bisexual, transsexual, and straight queerness. While we acknowledge that homosexuals as well as heterosexuals can operate or mediate from within straight cultural spaces and positions—after all, most of us grew up learning the rules of straight culture—we have paid less attention to the proposition that basically heterocentrist texts can contain queer elements, and basically heterosexual, straight-identifying people can experience queer moments. And these people should be encouraged to examine and express these moments *as* queer, not as moments of "homosexual panic," or temporary confusion, or as unfortunate, shameful, or sinful lapses in judgment or taste to be ignored, repressed, condemned, or somehow explained away within and by straight cultural politics—or even within and by gay or lesbian discourses.

My uses of the terms "queer readings," "queer discourses," and "queer positions," then, are attempts to account for the existence and expression of a wide range of positions within culture that are "queer" or non-, anti-, or contra-straight.[7] I am using the term "queer" to mark a flexible space for the expression of all aspects of non- (anti-, contra-) straight cultural production and reception.[8] As such, this cultural "queer space" recognizes the possibility that various and fluctuating queer positions might be occupied whenever *anyone* produces or responds to culture. In this sense, the use of the term "queer" to discuss reception takes up the standard binary opposition of "queer" and "nonqueer" (or "straight") while questioning its viability, at least in cultural studies, because, as noted earlier, the queer often operates within the nonqueer, as the nonqueer does within the queer (whether in reception, texts, or producers). The queer readings of mass culture I am concerned with in this essay will be those readings articulating positions *within* queer discourses. That is, these readings seem to be expressions of queer perspectives on mass culture from the inside, rather than descriptions of how "they" (gays and/or lesbians, usually) respond to, use, or are depicted in mass culture.

When a colleague heard I had begun using the word "queer" in my cultural studies work, she asked if I did so in order to "nostalgically" recapture and reassert the "romance" of the culturally marginal in the face of trends within straight capitalist societies to co-opt or contain aspects of queer cultures. I had, in fact, intended something quite different. By using "queer," I want to recapture and reassert a militant sense of difference that views the erotically "marginal" as both (in bell hooks's words) a consciously chosen "site of resistance" and a "location of radical openness and possibility."[9] And I want to suggest that within cultural production and reception, queer erotics are already part of culture's erotic center, both as a necessary construct by which to define the heterosexual and the straight (as "not queer"), and as a position that can be and is occupied in various ways by otherwise heterosexual and straight-identifying people.

But in another sense recapturing and reasserting a certain nostalgia and romance is part of my project here. For through playfully occupying various queer positions in relation to the fantasy/dream elements involved in cultural production and reception, we (whether straight-, gay-, lesbian-, or bi-identifying) are offered spaces to express a range of erotic desire frequently linked in Western cultures to nostalgic and romantic adult conceptions of childhood. Unfortunately, these moments of erotic complexity are usually explained away as part of the "regressive" work of mass media, whereby we are tricked into certain "unacceptable" and "immature" responses as passive subjects. But when cultural texts encourage straight-identified audience members to express a less-censored range of queer desire and pleasure than is possible in daily life, this "regression" has positive gender- and sexuality-destabilizing effects.[10]

I am aware of the current political controversy surrounding the word "queer." Some gays, lesbians, and bisexuals have expressed their inability to also identify with "queerness," as they feel the term has too long and too painful a history as a weapon of oppression and self-hate. These nonqueer lesbians, gays, and bisexuals find the attempts of radical forces in gay and lesbian communities (such as Queer Nation) to recover and positively redefine the term "queer" successful only within these communities—and unevenly successful at that. Preferring current or freshly created terms, non-queer-identifying lesbians, gays, and bisexuals often feel that any positive effects resulting from reappropriating "queer" are more theoretical than real.

But the history of gay and lesbian cultures and politics has shown that there are many times and places where the theoretical can have real social impact. Enough lesbians, gays, bisexuals, and other queers taking and making enough of these moments can create a more consistent awareness within the general public of queer cultural and political spaces, as these theory-in-the-flesh moments are concerned with making what has been for the most part publicly invisible and silent visible and vocal. In terms of mass culture reception, there are frequent theory-in-the-flesh opportunities in the course of everyday life. For example, how many times do we get the chance to inform people about our particular queer perspectives on film, television, literature, or music during conversations (or to engage someone else's perhaps unacknowledged queer perspective)? And how often, even if we are openly lesbian, gay, or bisexual, have we kept silent, or edited our conversations, deciding that our queer opinions are really only interesting to other queers, or that these opinions would make people uncomfortable—even while we think family, friends, and strangers should, of course, feel free to articulate various heterosexual or straight opinions in detail at any time?

Of course, queer positions aren't the only ones from which queers read and produce mass culture. As with nonqueers, factors such as class, ethnicity, gender, occupation, education, and religious, national, and regional allegiances influence our identity construction, and therefore are important to the positions we take as cultural producers and reader-consumers. These other cultural factors can exert influences difficult to separate from the development of our identities as queers, and as a result, difficult to discuss apart from our engagement in culture as queers. For example, most people find it next to impossible to articulate their sexual identities (queer or nonqueer) without some reference to gender. Generally, lesbian- and gay-specific forms of queer identities involve some degree of same-gender identification and desire or a cross-gender identification linked to same-gender desire. The understanding of what "gender" is in these cases can range from accepting conventional straight forms, which naturalize "feminine" and "masculine" by conflating them with essentializing, biology-based conceptions of "woman" and "man"; to imitating the outward forms and behaviors of one gender or the other while not fully subscribing to the straight ideological imperatives that define that gender; to combining or ignoring traditional gender codes in order to reflect attitudes that have little or nothing to do with straight ideas about femininity/women or masculinity/men. These last two positions are the places where queerly reconfigured gender identities begin to be worked out.[11]

"Begin to be," because most radically, as Sue-Ellen Case points out, "queer theory, unlike lesbian theory or gay male theory, is not gender specific."[12] Believing that "both gay and lesbian theory reinscribe sexual difference, to some extent, in their gender-specific constructions," Case calls for a queer theory that "works not at the site of gender, but at the site of ontology."[13] But while a nongendered notion of queerness makes sense, articulating this queer theory fully apart from gendered straight feminist, gay, and lesbian theorizing becomes difficult within languages and cultures that make gender and gender difference so crucial to their discursive practices. Through her discussions of vampire myths, Case works hard to establish a discourse that avoids gendered terms, yet she finds it necessary to resort to them every so often in order to suggest the queerness of certain things: placing "she" in quotation marks at one point, or discussing R. W. Fassbinder's film character Petra von Kant as "a truly queer creature who flickers somewhere between haute couture butch lesbian and male drag queen."[14]

Since I'm working with a conception of queerness that includes gay- and lesbian-specific positions as well as Case's nonlesbian and nongay queerness, gender definitions and uses here remain important to examining the ways in which queerness influences mass culture production and reception. For example, gay men who identify with some conception of "the feminine"[15] through processes that could stem from conscious personal choice, or from internalizing long-standing straight imperatives that encourage gay men to think of themselves as "not men" (and therefore, by implication or by direct attribution, as being like "women"), or from some degree of negotiation between these two processes, are at the center of the gay culture cults built around the imposing, spectacular women stars of opera (Maria Callas, Joan Sutherland, Beverly Sills, Renata Scotto, Teresa Stratas, Leontyne Price), theater (Lynn Fontanne, Katharine Cornell, Gertrude Lawrence, Maggie Smith, Angela Lansbury, Ethel Merman, Tallulah Bankhead), film (Bette Davis, Joan Crawford, Judy Garland, Marlene Dietrich, Vivien Leigh, Bette Midler, Glenda Jackson), popular music (Midler, Garland, Eartha Kitt, Edith Piaf, Barbra Streisand, Billie Holiday, Donna Summer, Diana Ross, Debbie Harry, Madonna), and television (Carol Burnett, the casts of *Designing Women* and *The Golden Girls*, Candice Bergen in *Murphy Brown*, Mary Tyler Moore and the supporting cast of women on *The Mary Tyler Moore Show*).[16] For the past two decades in the gay popular press, book chapters and articles on the connections between gay men and women stars have been a commonplace, but only occasionally do these works go beyond the monolithic audience label "gay men" to suggest the potential for discussing reception in a manner attuned to more specific definitions of sexual identity, such as those constructed to some degree within the dynamics of gender and sexuality.[17]

Given this situation, one strand of queer mass culture reception studies might be more precisely focused upon these networks of women performers who were, and are, meaningful at different times and places and for different reasons to feminine-identified gay men. One of most extended analytic pieces on feminine gay men's reception of women stars is the "Homosexuals' Girls" chapter of Julie Burchill's

Girls on Film. But Burchill is clearly writing critically *about* a particular queer reception position; she is not queerly positioned herself.
Indeed, Burchill's analysis of how "queens" respond to women stars
seems written to conform to very narrow-minded ideas about audience
and reception. For Burchill, all "feminine homosexual" men's investment in women stars is rooted in envy, jealousy, misogyny, and
cruelty—and she concludes this even as she relates a comment by
one of her gay friends: "You may have a flaming faggot's taste in movies, kid, but your perspective is pure Puritan."[18]

Clearly we need more popular and academic mass culture work
that carefully considers feminine gay and other gendered queer reception practices, as well as those of even less-analyzed queer readership
positions formed around the nexus of race and sexuality, or class and
sexuality, or ethnicity and sexuality, or some combination of gender/
race/class/ethnicity and sexuality.[19] These studies would offer valuable evidence of precisely how and where specific complex constructions of queerness can and do reveal themselves in the uses of mass
culture, as well as revealing how and where that mass culture comes
to influence and reinforce the process of queer identity formation.

One of the earliest attempts at such a study of queers and mass
culture was a series of interviews with nine lesbians conducted by
Judy Whitaker in 1981 for *Jump Cut*, "Hollywood Transformed."
These interviews touched upon a number of issues surrounding lesbian identity, including gender identification. Although careful to label these interviews "biographical sketches, not sociological or psychological studies," Whitaker does make some comments suggesting
the potential for such studies:

> Of the nine women who were interviewed, at least six said they
> identified at some time with male characters. Often the explanation is
> that men had the interesting active roles. Does this mean that these
> lesbians want to be like men? That would be a specious conclusion.
> None of the women who identified with male characters were "in love"
> with the characters' girl friends. All of the interviewees were "in love"
> at some time with actresses, but they did not identify with or want to
> be the male suitors of those actresses. While the context of the
> discussion is film, what these women are really talking about is their
> lives. . . . Transformation and positive self-image are dominant themes
> in what they have to say. Hollywood is transcended.[20]

After reading these interviews, there might be some question about
how fully the straight ideologies Hollywood narratives encourage are

"transcended" by these lesbian readers' uses of mainstream films, for as two of the interviewees remark, "We're so starved, we go see anything because something is better than nothing," and "It's a compromise. It's a given degree of alienation."[21] This sense of queer readings of mass culture as involving a measure of "compromise" and "alienation" contributes to the complexity of queer articulations of mass culture reception. For the pathos of feeling like a mass culture hanger-on is often related to the processes by which queers (and straights who find themselves queerly positioned) internalize straight culture's homophobic and heterocentrist attitudes and later reproduce them in their own queer responses to film and other mass culture forms.

Even so, traditional narrative films such as *Sylvia Scarlett*, *Gentlemen Prefer Blondes*, *Trapeze*, *To Live and Die in L.A.*, *Internal Affairs*, and *Thelma and Louise*, which are ostensibly addressed to straight audiences, often have greater potential for encouraging a wider range of queer responses than such clearly lesbian- and gay-addressed films as *Scorpio Rising*, *Home Movies*, *Women I Love*, and *Loads.*[22] The intense tensions and pleasures generated by the woman-woman and man-man aspects within the narratives of the former group of films create a space of sexual instability that already queerly positioned viewers can connect with in various ways, and within which straights might be likely to recognize and express their queer impulses. For example, gays might find a form of queer pleasure in the alternately tender and boisterous rapport between Lorelei/Marilyn Monroe and Dorothy/Jane Russell in *Gentlemen Prefer Blondes*, or in the exhilarating woman-bonding of the title characters in *Thelma and Louise*. Or lesbians and straights could queerly respond to the erotic elements in the relationships between the major male characters in *Trapeze*, *To Live and Die in L.A.*, or *Internal Affairs*. And any viewer might feel a sexually ambiguous attraction—is it gay, lesbian, bisexual, or straight?—to the image of Katharine Hepburn dressed as a young man in *Sylvia Scarlett*.

Of course, these queer positions and readings can become modified or can change over time, as people, cultures, and politics change. In my own case, as a white gay male who internalized dominant culture's definitions of myself as "like a woman" in a traditional 1950s and 1960s understanding of who "a woman" and what "femininity" was supposed to be, my pleasure in *Gentlemen Prefer Blondes* initially worked itself out through a classic gay process of identifying, alternately, with Monroe and Russell; thereby experiencing vicarious if temporary empowerment through their use of sexual allure to attract men—including the entire American Olympic team. Reassessing the feminine aspects of my gay sexual identity sometime in the 1970s (after Stonewall and my coming out), I returned to the film and discovered my response was now less rooted in the fantasy of being Monroe or Russell and gaining sexual access to men, than in the pleasure of Russell being the "gentleman" who preferred blonde Monroe, who looked out for her best interests, who protected her against men, and who enjoyed performing with her. This queer pleasure in a lesbian text has been abetted by extratextual information I have read, or was told, about Russell's solicitous and supportive offscreen behavior toward Monroe while making the film.[23] But along with these elements of queer reading that developed from the interaction of my feminine gay identity, my knowledge of extratextual behind-the-scenes gossip, and the text itself, I also take a great deal of direct gay erotic pleasure in the "Is There Anyone Here for Love?" number, enjoying its blatantly homo-historic and erotic ancient Greek Olympics mise-en-scène (including Russell's large column earrings), while admiring Russell's panache and good humor as she sings, strides, and strokes her way through a sea of half-naked male dancer-athletes. I no longer feel the need to mediate my sexual desires through her.

In 1985, Al LaValley suggested that this type of movement—from negotiating gay sexual desire through strong women stars to directly expressing desire for male images on screen—was becoming increasingly evident in gay culture, although certain forms of identification with women through gay connections with "the feminine" continue:

> One might have expected Stonewall to make star cults outmoded among gays. In a sense it did: The natural-man discourse, with its strong political and social vision and its sense of a fulfilled and open self, has supplanted both the aesthetic and campy discourses. . . . A delirious absorption in the stars is now something associated with pre-Stonewall gays or drag queens, yet neither gay openness nor the new machismo has completely abolished the cults. New figures are added regularly: Diana Ross, Donna Summer, Jennifer Holliday from the world of music, for example. There's a newer, more open gay following for male stars: Richard Gere, Christopher Reeve [and, to update, Mel Gibson], even teen hunks like Matt Dillon [Christopher Atkins, Johnny Depp, Jason Priestley, and Luke Perry].[24]

One could also add performers such as Bette Midler, Patti LaBelle, and Madonna to LaValley's list of women performers. While ambivalent about her motives ("Is she the Queen of Queers. . . . Or is she just milking us for shock value?"), Michael Musto's *Outweek* article "Immaculate Connection" suggests that Madonna is queer culture's post-Stonewall Judy Garland:

> By now, we finally seem willing to release Judy Garland from her afterlife responsibility of being our quintessential icon. And in the land of the living, career stagnation has robbed Diana [Ross], Liza [Minnelli], and Barbra [Streisand] of their chances, while Donna [Summer] thumped the bible on our heads in a way that made it bounce back into her face. That leaves Madonna as Queer Queen, and she merits the title as someone who isn't afraid to offend straight America if it does the rest of us some good.[25]

Musto finds Madonna "unlike past icons" as she's "not a vulnerable toy"; this indicates to him the need to reexamine gay culture's enthusiasms for women stars with greater attention to how shifting historic (and perhaps generational) contexts alter the meanings and uses of these stars for particular groups of gay men.[26]

Examining how and where these gay cults of women stars work in relation to what LaValley saw in the mid-1980s as the "newer, more openly gay following for male stars" would also make for fascinating cultural history. Certainly there have been "homosexual" followings for male personalities in mass culture since the late nineteenth century, with performers and actors—Sandow the muscleman, Edwin Booth—vying with gay enthusiasms for opera divas and actresses such as Jenny Lind and Lillian Russell. Along these lines, one could queerly combine star studies with genre studies in order to analyze the gay appreciation of women musical performers, and the musical's "feminine" or "effeminized" aesthetic, camp, and emotive genre characteristics (spectacularized decor and costuming, intricate choreography, and singing about romantic yearning and fulfillment), with reference to the more hidden cultural history of gay erotics centered around men in musicals.[27]

In film, this erotic history would perhaps begin with Ramon Navarro (himself gay) stripped down to sing "Pagan Love Song" in *The Pagan*. Beyond this, a gay beefcake musical history would include Gene Kelly (whose ass was always on display in carefully tailored pants); numbers like "Is There Anyone Here for Love?" (*Gentlemen Prefer Blondes*) and "Y.M.C.A." (*Can't Stop the Music*) that feature men in gym shorts, swimsuits (Esther Williams musicals are especially spectacular in this regard), military (especially sailor) uniforms, and pseudo-native or pseudo-classical (Greek and Roman) out-fits; films such as *Athena* (bodybuilders), *Seven Brides for Seven Brothers* (Western Levis, flannel, and leather men), *West Side Story* (Hispanic and Anglo t-shirted and blue-jeaned delinquents, includ-ing a butch girl); Elvis Presley films (and those of other "teen girl" pop and rock music idols—Frank Sinatra, Ricky Nelson, Fabian, Cliff Richard, the Beatles, and so on); and the films of John Travolta (*Saturday Night Fever, Grease, Staying Alive*), Patrick Swayze (*Dirty Dancing*), and Mikhail Baryshnikov, who in *The Turning Point and White Nights* provided the impetus for many gays to be more vocal about their "lowbrow" sexual pleasure in supposedly high-cultural male bodies. If television, music video, and concert performers and texts were added to this hardly exhaustive list, it would include David Bowie, Morrissey, David Cassidy, Tom Jones, and Marky Mark, among many others, and videos such as *Cherish, Express Yourself,* and *Justify My Love* (all performed by Madonna), *Being Boring* (The Pet Shop Boys), *Love Will Never Do Without You* (Janet Jackson), *Just Tell Me That You Want Me* (Kim Wilde), and *Rico Suave* (Gerardo), along with a number of heavy-metal videos featuring long-haired lead sing-ers in a variety of skintight and artfully opened or ripped clothes.[28]

I can't leave this discussion of gay erotics and musicals without a few more words about Gene Kelly's "male trio" musicals, such as *On the Town, Take Me Out to the Ball Game,* and *It's Always Fair Weather.*[29] Clad in sailor uniforms, baseball uniforms, and Army uni-forms, the male trios in these films are composed of two convention-ally sexy men (Kelly and Frank Sinatra in the first two films, Kelly and Dan Dailey in the last) and a comic, less attractive "buffer" (Jules Munshin in the first two, Michael Kidd in the last) who is meant to diffuse the sexual energy generated between the two male leads when they sing and dance together. Other Kelly films—*Singin' in the Rain, An American in Paris,* and *Anchors Aweigh*—resort to the more con-ventional heterosexual(izing) narrative device of using a woman to mediate and diffuse male-male erotics.[30] But whether in the form of a third man or an ingenue, these devices fail to fully heterosexualize the relationship between Kelly and his male costars. In *Singin' in the Rain*, for example, I can't help but read Donald O'Connor maniacally unleashing his physical energy to entertain Kelly during the "Make 'Em Laugh" number as anything but a case of overwrought, displaced gay desire.[31]

Kelly himself jokingly refers to the queer erotics of his image and his many buddy musicals in *That's Entertainment!*, when he reveals

the answer to the often-asked question, "Who was your favorite dancing partner . . . Cyd Charisse, Leslie Caron, Rita Hayworth, Vera-
Ellen?," by showing a clip of the dance he did with Fred Astaire
("The Babbit and the Bromide") in *Ziegfeld Follies*. "It's the only time
we danced together," Kelly remarks over the clip, "but I'd change my
name to Ginger if we could do it again." As it turned out, Kelly and
Astaire did "do it again" in *That's Entertainment 2*, and their reunion
as a dancing couple became the focus of much of the film's publicity
campaign, as had been the case when Astaire reunited with Ginger
Rogers in *The Barkleys of Broadway*.[32]

While there has been at the very least a general, if often clichéd,
cultural connection made between gays and musicals, lesbian work
within the genre has been less acknowledged. However, the evidence
of lesbian viewing practices — in articles such as "Hollywood Transformed," in videos such as *Dry Kisses Only* (1990, Jane Cottis and
Kaucyila Brooke) and *Grapefruit* (1989, Cecilia Dougherty), and in
informal discussions (mention *Calamity Jane* to a group of thirty- to
forty-something American lesbians) — suggests that lesbian viewers
have always negotiated their own culturally specific readings and
pleasures within the genre.[33] Although it never uses the word "lesbian," Lucie Arbuthnot and Gail Seneca's 1982 article "Pre-text and
Text in *Gentlemen Prefer Blondes*" is perhaps the best-known les-
bian-positioned piece on the musical. While couched in homosocial
rhetoric, this analysis of the authors' pleasures in the film focuses
upon Lorelei/Monroe's and Dorothy/Russell's connection to each
other through looks, touch, and words ("lovey," "honey," "sister,"
"dear"). Noting that a "typical characteristic of [the] movie musical
genre is that there are two leads, a man and a woman, who sing and
dance together, and eventually become romantically involved," Seneca and Arbuthnot recognize that in *Gentlemen Prefer Blondes* "it is
Monroe and Russell who sing — and even harmonize, adding another
layer to the metaphor — and dance as a team."[34] Since the men in the
film are "never given a musical role," the authors conclude "the pre-
text of heterosexual romance is so thin that it scarcely threatens the
text of female friendship."[35]

One note hints at a possible butch-femme reading of the Russell/
Monroe relationship, centered upon Russell's forthright stride and
stance: "The Russell character also adopts a 'masculine' stride and
stance. More often, Monroe plays the 'lady' to Russell's manly moves.
For example, Russell opens doors for Monroe; Monroe sinks into Russell's strong frame, allowing Russell to hold her protectively."[36] Re-

leased in 1953, during the height of traditional butch-femme role-playing in American urban lesbian culture, *Gentlemen Prefer Blondes* could well have been read and enjoyed by lesbians at the time with reference to this particular social-psychological paradigm for understanding and expressing their sexual identity.[37] The film continues to be read along these lines by some lesbians as well as by other queerly positioned viewers. Overall, Seneca and Arbuthnot's analysis of *Gentlemen Prefer Blondes* qualifies as a lesbian reading, as it discusses the film and the musical genre so as to "re-vision . . . connections with women" by focusing upon the pleasures of and between women on the screen and women in the audience, rather than on "the ways in which the film affords pleasure, or denies pleasure, to men."[38]

Working with the various suggestive comments in this article and considering actual and potential lesbian readings of other musicals can lead to a consideration of other pairs and trios of song-and-dance women performers (often related as sisters in the narratives), certain strong solo women film and video musical stars (Eleanor Powell, Esther Williams, Carmen Miranda, Lena Horne, Eartha Kitt, Doris Day, Julie Andrews, Tina Turner, Madonna), and musical numbers performed by groups of women, with little or no participation by men.[39] Of particular interest in this latter category are those often-reviled Busby Berkeley musical spectacles, which appear in a different light if one considers lesbians (and other queers) as spectators, rather than straight men. I'm thinking here especially of numbers like "The Lady in the Tutti-Frutti Hat" in *The Gang's All Here*, where Carmen Miranda triggers an all-woman group masturbation fantasia involving banana dildos and foot fetishism; "Dames" in *Dames*, where women sleep, bathe, dress, and seek employment together — some pause to acknowledge the camera as bearer of the voyeuristic (straight) male gaze, only to prohibit this gaze by using powder puffs, atomizer sprays, and other objects to cover the lens; "The Polka-Dot Ballet" in *The Gang's All Here*, where androgynized women in tights rhythmically move neon hoops and large dots in unison, then melt into a vivid, hallucinogenically colored vaginal opening initially inhabited by Alice Faye's head surrounded by shiny cloth; "Spin a Little Web of Dreams" in *Fashions of 1934*, where a seamstress falls asleep and "spins a little web of dreams" about a group of seminude women amid giant undulating ostrich-feather fans who, at one point, create a tableau called "Venus with Her Galley Slaves"; and parts of many other numbers (the two women sharing an upper berth on the Niagara Limited who cynically comment upon marriage in *42nd Street*'s "Shuffle Off to Buffalo," for example).[40]

Since this discussion of queer positions and queer readings seems to have worked itself out so far largely as a discussion of musical stars and the musical genre, I might add here that of the articles and books written about film musicals only the revised edition of Jane Feuer's *Hollywood Musicals* goes beyond a passing remark in considering the ways in which this genre has been the product of gay film workers, or how the ways in which musicals are viewed and later talked about have been influenced by gay and lesbian reception practices.[41] From most accounts of the musical, it is a genre whose celebration of heterosexual romance must always be read straight. The same seems to be the case with those other film genres typically linked to gays, lesbians, and bisexuals: the horror/fantasy film and the melodrama. While there has been a rich history of queers producing and reading these genres, surprisingly little has been done to formally express this cultural history. There has been more queer work done in and on the horror film: vampire pieces by Richard Dyer, Bonnie Zimmerman, and Sue-Ellen Case; Bruna Fionda, Polly Gladwin, Isiling Mack-Nataf's lesbian vampire film *The Mark of Lilith* (1986); Amy Goldstein's vampire musical film *Because the Dawn* (1988); a sequence in *Dry Kisses Only* that provides a lesbian take on vampire films; an article by Martin F. Norden on sexuality in *The Bride of Frankenstein*; and some pieces on *The Rocky Horror Picture Show* (although most are not written from a queer position), to cite a few examples.[42]

But there is still much left unexamined beyond the level of conversation. Carl Dreyer's lesbophobic "classic" *Vampyr* could use a thorough queer reading, as could Tod Browning's *Dracula*—which opens with a coach ride through Transylvania in the company of a superstitious Christian straight couple, a suit-and-tie lesbian couple, and a feminine gay man, who will quickly become the bisexual Count Dracula's vampirized servant. Subsequent events in the film include a straight woman who becomes a child molester known as "The Woman in White" after the count vampirizes her. It is also amazing that gay horror director James Whale has yet to receive full-scale queer auteurist consideration for films such as *Frankenstein* (the idea of men making the "perfect" man), *The Bride of Frankenstein* (gay Dr. Praetorius; queer Henry Frankenstein; the erotics between the blind man, the monster, and Jesus on the cross; the overall campy atmosphere), *The Old Dark House* (a gay and lesbian brother and sister; a 103-year-old man in the attic who is actually a woman), and *The In-*

visible Man (effete, mad genius Claude Rains spurns his fiancée, becomes invisible, tries to find a male partner in crime, and becomes
visible only after he is killed by the police).[43] Beyond queer readings
of specific films and directors, it would also be important to consider
how the central conventions of horror and melodrama actually encourage queer positioning as they exploit the spectacle of heterosexual romance, straight domesticity, and traditional gender roles gone awry.
In a sense, then, *everyone's* pleasure in these genres is "perverse," is
queer, as much of it takes place within the space of the contra-heterosexual and the contra-straight.

   Just how much everyone's pleasures in mass culture are part of this
contra-straight, rather than strictly antistraight, space—just how
queer our responses to cultural texts are so much of the time—is what
I'd finally like this chapter to suggest. Queer positions, queer readings, and queer pleasures are part of a reception space that stands
simultaneously beside and within that created by heterosexual and
straight positions. These positions, readings, and pleasures also suggest that what happens in cultural reception goes beyond the traditional opposition of homo and hetero, as queer reception is often a
place beyond the audience's conscious "real-life" definition of their
sexual identities and cultural positions—often, but not always, beyond such sexual identities and identity politics, that is. For in all my
enthusiasm for breaking down rigid concepts of sexuality through the
example of mass culture reception, I don't want to suggest that there is
a queer utopia that unproblematically and apolitically unites straights
and queers (or even all queers) in some mass culture reception area in
the sky. Queer reception doesn't stand outside personal and cultural
histories; it is part of the articulation of these histories. This is why,
politically, queer reception (and production) practices can include everything from the reactionary to the radical to the indeterminate, as
with the audience for (as well as the producers of) "queercore" publications, who individually and collectively often seem to combine reactionary and radical attitudes.

   What queer reception often does, however, is stand outside the relatively clear-cut and essentializing categories of sexual identity under
which most people function. You might identify yourself as a lesbian
or a straight woman yet queerly experience the gay erotics of male
buddy films such as *Red River* and *Butch Cassidy and the Sundance
Kid*; or maybe as a gay man your cultlike devotion to *Laverne and
Shirley, Kate and Allie*, or *The Golden Girls* has less to do with
straight-defined cross-gender identification than with your queer en-

joyment in how these series are crucially concerned with articulating the loving relationships between women.[44] Queer readings aren't "alternative" readings, wishful or willful misreadings, or "reading too much into things" readings. They result from the recognition and articulation of the complex range of queerness that has been in popular culture texts and their audiences all along.

CHAPTER TWO

Whose Text Is It Anyway?

Queer Cultures, Queer Auteurs, and Queer Authorship

There is a moment in George Cukor's 1939 film *The Women* that I will use as a condensed illustration of the critical issues in this chapter. The scene is a luncheon at Mary Haines's suburban home. As Mary passes biscuits around, Sylvia Fowler refuses them because she is watching her weight. "Go ahead, dear. No starch, it's gluten!" Mary exclaims. Taking a biscuit, Sylvia sarcastically remarks to the other women: "Have you ever known such a housewife?" In a film abounding with in-jokes, this moment is perhaps the slyest and the most subversive of them all. For Sylvia is played by Rosalind Russell, who three years earlier had portrayed the neurotically "perfect" housewife Harriet Craig in *Craig's Wife*, directed by Dorothy Arzner.[1]

Linked by an actress who was to become a cult favorite for many lesbians and gays, Cukor's reference to Arzner pivots on an implicitly antidomestic wisecrack pertinent to the hidden agenda of both *Craig's Wife* and *The Women*, as well as to that of a number of Arzner and Cukor films. In terms of queer cultural history, Russell's retort also offers itself as a hidden homage by one queer director to another—that is, if you know Cukor was homosexual (Cukor disliked the term "gay") and Arzner was lesbian.[2] With this queer biographical information, the moment of closeted comradeship in *The Women* becomes both touching and provocative, placed as it is within the context of a conventional narrative film produced by a capitalist industry for a straight society.

The genesis of the following thoughts on Cukor, Arzner, auteurism, authorship, queerness, and queer cultures was an invitation to present a paper at a Cukor and Arzner symposium that was part of the 1990 Pittsburgh Lesbian and Gay Film Festival. The particular context for this lecture suggested that I consider traditional auteurist notions of Arzner and Cukor as queer directors expressing consistent, idiosyncratic stylistic and thematic concerns throughout the body of their films, as well as questions of how Cukor, Arzner, and their films might be meaningful in and for queer cultures, particularly lesbian and gay ones. Thinking about the critical approaches implied by this public context for the paper, the anecdotal cross-referencing of Cukor's *The Women* and Arzner's *Craig's Wife* seemed to point out how the demands of established critical approaches such as auteurism and other types of authorship studies might require reworking when set against the work of queer cultures and queer cultural analysis.[3]

In this chapter, I use the terms "auteur," "auteurism," and "auteurist" with reference to traditional and revisionist critical work that was initially concerned with questions about directors and how central they might be in controlling or otherwise influencing the form and meanings of cultural texts (usually films, although sometimes videos, television programs, and television commercials). A "strong" auteur will develop a recognizable style and thematics that are carried from text to text, creating an oeuvre that expresses a consistent personal aesthetic and ideology. A "weaker" director—traditionally called a "stylist," a "metteur-en-scène," or a "hack"—exerts limited or erratic influence over her or his projects.

Classic *Cahiers du Cinema* "politiques des auteurs" statements as well as the "auteur theory" popularized by Andrew Sarris were re-examined in the late 1960s and throughout the 1970s from various structuralist, poststructuralist, and feminist theoretical positions. The resulting reworkings of traditional auteurism often reconceptualized the director as a set of textual codes, signs, or structures named after the actual person, but not to be confused with them ("Howard Hawks" rather than Howard Hawks, for example). In addition, theorists and critical commentators offered alternative auteurs—stars, writers, and cinematographers—or developed the notion of multiple or group auteurs in order to question what they saw as the myth of hegemonic directorial auteurship in what is usually collaborative mass culture production. Simultaneously, theorists such as Roland Barthes opened critical spaces by suggesting that readers do their share in "authoring" the meanings of texts from their positions as cultural consumers.[4]

Currently, auteurs and auteurism are often invoked in mass culture studies within more general discussions of "authorship," a term I understand as indicating a more open and flexible approach to the attribution of influence and meaning in mass culture texts. Auteurs and auteurism might be said to specifically concern the production context of mass culture (directors, stars, producers, writers, cinematographers, etc.), while "authors" and "authorship" can be employed to discuss circumstances of production, exhibition (including promotion), or reception. Given this, attributing authorship—establishing the credit for important and significant influences upon the form and the meanings of cultural texts—remains contested ground, as production records, interviews, (auto)biographies, official and unofficial credits, publicity, and various cultural reception practices will frequently be at odds in establishing the authorship of a text.

The claims of authorship are both simplified and complicated when examining Arzner's and Cukor's films within the context of queer cultural studies, as both directors were homosexual. While presenting papers about Arzner and Cukor and screening their films make obvious auteurist sense at a retrospective or at an academic symposium, does doing so in the context of a queer cultural event make as much self-evident sense? Why should queers bother with Cukor and Arzner? If career survival and success within the Hollywood system were the issue, why not focus on a Howard Hawks or an Alfred Hitchcock, whose bodies of work have the added advantage of containing more obvious queerly erotic and crypto-queer elements than are readily apparent in all the films of Cukor and Arzner—excepting, perhaps, *Sylvia Scarlett*. Being erotically attracted to members of their own sex shouldn't automatically make these directors interesting to queer cultures. Indeed, a radical queer critique of Cukor and Arzner as auteurs would say that they were closeted homosexual collaborators who helped perpetuate a heterocentrist industry catering to the desires of a queer-oppressive society.

But while there may be something to this, there are ways in which the lives and works of Dorothy Arzner and George Cukor have been, and might continue to be, analyzed within the context of queer culture and queer cultural studies. Beyond this, a spectator's queer pleasure in Arzner and Cukor texts can be enriched by considering a critical approach that combines auteurism and queer cultural reception practices.

Relatively recent work to discover (and create) queer history in order to make it more visible (including the strategy of "outing") has encouraged discussions exploring the relationship of sexual orientation to cultural creation and production. It is important to recall, however, that these discussions have always been encouraged in queer cultures through the "guess who's lesbian, gay, or bisexual?" gossip grapevine. This informal and vital source of information has, for a number of decades, encouraged many gays, lesbians, bisexuals, and even some straights to develop their own specifically queer forms of auteurist analyses around certain cultural figures and their creative output.

Gay culture—and by this I mean, in this case, a gay culture fostered largely by white middle- and upper-class urban men—discovered individual Cukor and Arzner films before they recognized Arzner and Cukor as auteurs, or as queers/queer auteurs. Generally, gay cultural enthusiasm for these films was first generated and sustained through the women stars in them: Greta Garbo in *Camille* and *Two-Faced Woman*; Katharine Hepburn in *Little Women*, *Christopher Strong*, *Sylvia Scarlett*, and *Adam's Rib*, among other films; Jean Harlow in *Dinner at Eight*; Clara Bow in *The Wild Party*; Judy Garland in *A Star Is Born*; Joan Crawford in *The Women*, *A Woman's Face*, and *The Bride Wore Red*; Ruth Chatterton in *Sarah and Son*; and Rosalind Russell in *Craig's Wife* and *The Women*.[5] This being the case, gay cultural readings of these Cukor and Arzner films were (and still are) often worked out within star-as-auteur paradigms. That is, these readings are primarily concerned with analyzing, and actually helping to create, the meanings of a star's image across films by different directors. An important part of such star-as-text/text-as-"star vehicle" reading practices is using extratextual material: exploitation and marketing information (reviews, interviews, advertising, studio publicity), gossip, and even fantasies and fictions created around the stars.

Most of the stars and films I've just mentioned could also be cited as examples of how many lesbians first came to appreciate films directed by Arzner and Cukor. Through their own star-as-auteur cultural readings, lesbians developed cults for Garbo and Hepburn, for example.[6] An issue of the lesbian and gay quarterly OUT/LOOK contains a tribute to Garbo by the artist Margie Adams that begins: "Garbo is dead. And the grief that sits in the corner of my day is, first of all, simple. I have loved and admired her since the first time I saw her in 1964, in *Grand Hotel*. I was seventeen, an awkward, fierce, and angular young one, just come out three months earlier, and I knew, right down to my molecular structure, that the shimmering beauty with such a jawline up there on the screen was a dyke, just like me."[7]

Since erotic pleasure and identification are so central to these lesbian star cults, I would guess most lesbians who love such Cukor films as *Camille, Little Women, Sylvia Scarlett,* or *Adam's Rib* finally care very little that the same person directed all these films, even once they discover this person was a self-defined homosexual. Aside from perhaps taking some degree of incidental pleasure in the knowledge that a queer worked with Garbo and Hepburn on these films, I doubt most lesbian readings and uses of the films I've just cited are fundamentally concerned with director-as-auteur, or even director-as-queer-auteur considerations.

The situation might be different in Arzner's case, as knowing another lesbian was involved in the presentation of a figure of identification and erotic desire such as Hepburn is bound to encourage lesbian viewers to reexamine the films for signs of the director's narrative and stylistic articulation of lesbian desires and attitudes in relation to the star. And, of course, as knowledge of Arzner's queerness is becoming more widespread, her life and works are becoming important in lesbian (and more generally queer) cultural readings of film history, as well as in individual lesbian/queer readings of Arzner films. One can reverse these observations about Arzner and Cukor in relation to gays and gay cultural history. Whereas discovering Arzner was queer would not fundamentally alter most readings of those films gays had come to through star cults, or perhaps through genre cults (such as for maternal melodramas and musicals), knowing Cukor was gay could make a great difference to gay readings of his films, and to articulating gay cultural history in general. To mention just one instance, the critical commonplace about Cukor being a "woman's director" would take on different meanings when placed within the context of certain cross-gender identification practices in gay culture.[8]

Of course, an important consideration in all this formal and informal queer cultural work is the intersection of cultural history and the personal history of the reader. It is in this intersection that queers have mapped out the complex and diverse space of their interactions with mass culture. We enter cultural history at various times and under differing circumstances, which affect how we make sense of the personalities and products within a culture. For example, in earlier periods lesbians might initially become acquainted with the films of Garbo or Arzner through erotic attraction, lesbian star cult, or feminist scholarship, and they would develop readings and uses of Garbo and Arzner through these approaches. More recently, lesbians might first come to Garbo and Arzner upon hearing something about their lesbianism (or alleged lesbianism), information that might then develop into the central analytic focus for these viewers' appreciation of the star's and the director's films as "lesbian films." This reading process uses extratextual material as a way of "author-izing" the decoding and reading of certain narrative and style codes in films as specific to lesbian culture.[9]

Naturally, as audiences move through history as individuals and as members of groups, their initial readings and uses of culture are subject to additions and revisions. A recent piece on Arzner's films that examines earlier academic feminist work in the light of specifically lesbian critical perspectives is Judith Mayne's "Female Authorship Reconsidered" in *The Woman at the Keyhole*.[10] In this chapter, Mayne suggests that the central marks of Arzner's "female authorship" are to be found in the tensions between her narrative interest in female communities and friendships among women and her representations of herself through certain secondary characters coded as "mannish" lesbians. In relation to this, Mayne proposes that "textually, the most pervasive sign of Arzner's authorship is her use of irony." This irony takes the form of a general female/feminist "ironic perspective on patriarchal institutions," as well as more specific forms of "lesbian irony." Both of these ironic modes work to reinforce those tensions between the homosocial and the erotic Arzner develops in her films' narratives and characterizations.[11]

But aside from Mayne, and academic conference papers by Jane Gaines and Claudia Gorbman, most writers have ignored Arzner's sexual biography and its potential relevance to lesbian and queer cultures in terms of questions of authorship. Indeed, until feminist academics interviewed her in the mid-1970s, no one was much interested in Arzner's life at all. And because Arzner resisted discussing herself as a feminist or as a lesbian, even this one interview, conducted by Karyn Kay and Gerald Peary, carefully avoids the topic of Arzner's sexuality and how it may have influenced her work.[12] In spite of Arzner's hesitancy, though, the interviewers do constantly return to a straight feminist agenda, often asking Arzner to discuss what it was like to be a woman working within the studio system, or about the ways in which she may have paid more attention to coaching actresses and developing women characters.

However, there is a moment in this interview where Arzner, consciously or not, offers an opportunity for a discussion of cross-gender identification within erotic narrative situations as one means of establishing a lesbian mode of expression within traditional film forms. This moment comes when Arzner deflects another attempt to link her identification to the actresses and women characters in *Christopher Strong*: "But I was more interested in Christopher Strong, played by Colin Clive, than in any of the women characters. He was a man 'on the cross.' He loved his wife, and he fell in love with the aviatrix. He was on a rack. I was really more sympathetic with him, but no one seemed to pick up on that."[13] Understandably, the straight, auteur-as-feminist program of Arzner's interviewers kept them from pursuing the potential auteur-as-lesbian coding in this statement.

Unlike Arzner, George Cukor was interviewed many times by journalists and scholars outside the Hollywood publicity machine, once at book length. The continued availability of this material has allowed the interested general public to indulge in some form of biographical (if not necessarily queer) auteurist readings of Cukor films. Cukor also has the advantage of an interview with Boze Hadleigh that touched upon issues of sexual identity and creative production within the Hollywood system. This interview, reprinted in Hadleigh's book *Conversations with My Elders*, became part of Cukor's personal and professional coming out.[14] This process was continued after Cukor's death with Patrick McGilligan's *George Cukor: A Double Life*, which considers the director's personal life and professional life within particular gay cultural contexts, with reference to Cukor's own attitudes about his "homosexuality."[15]

In "Authorship and Cukor: A Reappraisal," one of the first academic articles on the director after his coming out, Richard Lippe takes issue with earlier auteurist critics who devalued Cukor's authorship by pejoratively categorizing him as a "woman's director" or a "stylist." While Lippe makes clear his desire to "indicate why [he] think[s] Cukor deserves recognition as an auteur," he also suggests that his interest in reevaluating Cukor's films isn't only focused on "their status as auteurist works" by a gay man. From his position as a gay cultural critic, Lippe is also concerned with how Cukor's films and his career are "relevant to a discussion of the Hollywood cinema which remains to the present-day a homophobic institution," as well as how Cukor's films examine "an extremely crude and barbaric social and economic system . . . which is constructed on sexual inequality."[16]

In setting up their critical and theoretical apparatus for analyzing Arzner and Cukor as auteurs, both Lippe and Mayne provide insightful critical surveys of the work done on authorship (as a general topic and with reference to these directors) to that point. Lippe's ultimate "commitment to a modified form of auteurism in which the director,

as [Robin] Wood puts it, functions as an 'intervention' in the construction of the text" is a move to restore some recognition of the "creative
subjectivity" of cultural producers in order to develop "richer and
more nuanced readings which, in turn, contribute to a better understanding of the spectator's own subjectivity as social and sexual being."[17] While criticizing classic auteurism on both sides of the Atlantic for canonizing only those directors expressing traditionally
masculine themes and styles, Mayne also finds the auteurism of many
early feminists limited by an implicitly straight gender ideology that
often resulted in criticism that searched for some vague "idealized ab-
straction" of female authorship "as agency and self-representation"
even while working within auteurist paradigms that saw female authorship, at best, "as a negative inflection of the norms of classical
[male-dominated] cinema."[18] In reading Arzner's work, Mayne opts
for a "both/and" approach to discussing the director's auteurism that
acknowledges that her films contain the signs of patriarchal aesthetics
and ideology and, at the same time, become the site for directly articulating her feminist-lesbian concerns.[19]

In constructing an auteurism to fit their gay and lesbian critical
agendas, Lippe and Mayne reveal some of the range of approaches
available to queers in developing forms of authorship that consider
how ideas and information about directors (or other important creative
collaborators), whether they are queer themselves or not, have been,
are, and might be significant in queer cultural readings of individual
texts and bodies of work. This would be a use of auteurism that considers that meanings are constructed within and across film texts
through the interplay of creators, cultures, and audiences. As a result, queer auteurs could either be "born" or "made"; that is, a case
could be developed for directors (or stars, or scriptwriters, etc.) as
queer auteurs on the basis of their being queer (Cukor, Arzner,
Mitchell Leisen, Isaac Julien, Sergei Eisenstein, Richard Fung, Edmund Goulding, Marlon Riggs, F. W. Murnau, James Whale,
Michelle Parkerson, Luchino Visconti, Ulrike Ottinger, Barbara
Hammer, Kenneth Anger, R. W. Fassbinder, and many others), or on
the evidence that many of their films hold, or have held, particularly
meaningful places within queer cultural history, with or without
knowledge of the director's sexuality (Cukor again, Vincente Minnelli, Alfred Hitchcock, William Wyler, Josef von Sternberg, Leontine Sagan, Ernst Lubitsch, Max Ophuls, Douglas Sirk, Rouben
Mamoulian, Billy Wilder, Susan Seidelman, Joseph L. Mankiewicz,
Busby Berkeley, and others). Perhaps another way queer auteurs are

"made" happens when the films of non-queer-identified directors become interesting to queerly positioned spectators for their queer (sub)texts (Hitchcock, Seidelman, Jacques Rivette, Diane Kurys, Howard Hawks, Martin Scorcese, Carol Reed, Nicholas Ray, Blake Edwards, Joseph Losey, and others). Of course, there is always the possibility of queerly reading the oeuvre of any director (star, scriptwriter, etc.) by conducting a queer analysis of textual discourses articulating sexual desire and sexual identity, whether these concern queer or non-queer subjects.

As part of queer cultural authorship practices that employ some form of auteurism to establish queer auteurs, queers might borrow the notion from Andrew Sarris and other early auteurists that certain unconventional elements of a director's biography and ideology could be expressed within the conventional texts of a capitalist industry — even if sporadically and in heavily coded forms. To this we might add *Cahiers du Cinema*'s structuralist reworking of auteurism in 1969, which separates films into seven categories, "a" to "g." Each category is defined according to how clearly and coherently a culture's ideological agenda is conveyed through the text. Of particular interest for queer auteurist readings of Arzner and Cukor films is Category "e," which is defined as containing films in which

> an internal criticism is taking place which cracks the film apart at the seams. If one reads the film obliquely, looking for symptoms; if one looks beyond the apparent formal coherence, one can see that it is riddled with cracks. . . . This is the case in many Hollywood films, for example, which while being completely integrated into the system and the ideology end up by partially dismantling the system from within.[20]

Viewed as Category "e" films, the works of many commercial directors, but even more those of queer directors such as Cukor and Arzner, might be "obliquely" examined by queer-positioned readers for textual signs that complicate or resist the coherent presentation of conventional straight ideology.

Finally, feminist work with auteurism in the 1970s and 1980s provides queer spectators and critics with analytic models linking auteurist analysis to the articulation of certain theories and polemics. Implicitly basing many of their readings of traditional narrative films on the *Cahiers* Category "e" paradigm, feminist critics would search the works of directors such as Raoul Walsh, Alfred Hitchcock, and Dorothy Arzner for textual gaps, contradictions, and excesses around which to construct radical readings of these director's works from positions critiquing patriarchal ideology.

As part of this feminist auteurism, studio directors such as Arzner, Ida Lupino, Lois Weber, and Alice Guy-Blaché were rediscovered and their careers and works reread as part of a feminist project to construct their own film history, film theory, and film practice. To this end, feminist uses of auteurism initially concentrated upon identifying "female discourses" within and between the films of female (and a few male) directors. Although critically examining the production contexts in which these directors worked was important to feminist auteurist readings, as they exposed various institutional and aesthetic impediments to directly expressing female discourses in film, the personal biographies of directors appeared to hold little interest for the first wave of feminist commentators, aside from these directors' status as (implicitly straight) "women" or "men."

But since queerness is not usually visible in the ways gender is understood to be, biographical information about directors (and stars, writers, etc.) and spectators often becomes crucial to examining queer authorship. For queer people on all sides of the camera—before it, behind it, and in the audience—the problem of expressing ourselves from our positions as invisible and oppressed "minority" sexual cultures within a hypervisible and pervasive straight culture offers a compelling parallel to auteurist notions that certain studio directors expressed their unconventional views by developing oppositional practices within conventional production and narrative models. The signs of such oppositional practices, whether intentional or not, would be found in those elements of textual tension and contradiction created through formal emphases—whether narrative or stylistic.[21]

Following this line, we can say that directors—and certainly queer directors—who had particularly unspeakable ideological programs found it necessary to continue developing a repertoire of sly working-within-the-system expressive tactics even once they achieved stature within the industry. Arzner and Cukor were among those commercially successful studio directors who eventually attained a degree of creative choice and collaborative control in developing their projects. This could mean making casting suggestions, as well as influencing the choice of scenarist, cinematographer, and other crew members. Perhaps this explains such daring projects as Cukor's *Sylvia Scarlett* and Arzner's *Christopher Strong*, as well as startling moments such as Maureen O'Hara's class- and patriarchy-dismantling, working woman-bonding speech in Arzner's *Dance, Girl, Dance*; young Mary's comment as she jumps in bed with her mother in *The Women*: "You know, that's the one good thing about divorce—you get to sleep with your mother"; Clara Bow's "You see, I love her too," in *The Wild Party*; or the last line of *Our Betters*, delivered by a heavily made-up fop observing the reconciliation of two socialites: "Ah, what an exquisite spectacle! Two ladies of title kissing one another."[22]

Apart from *Sylvia Scarlett*, these films and scenes almost, but don't quite, openly express queer positions within conventional narrative texts. These particular Cukor and Arzner films do invite spectators to view "obliquely" the conventions of straight narrative construction and the straight ideology these narratives attempt to naturalize. As such, they become crucial in developing queerly authored auteurist readings of Arzner's and Cukor's films. In order to more vividly illustrate how some of the ideas about queer auteurism outlined above might be combined with those other forms of queer cultural authorship mentioned earlier, I offer the following brief comments on *Christopher Strong*; *Dance, Girl, Dance*; *Camille*; and *Sylvia Scarlett*.

Even without knowing about Arzner's identification with *Christopher Strong*'s central male character, who is caught in a love triangle with Katharine Hepburn and Billie Burke, there is much in this film to encourage queer director and star auteurist readings. Hepburn's personality and image, perhaps, are at the center of it all. If viewers remember nothing else about this film, they usually recall two images of Hepburn. The first one has her clad in various versions of a pilot's outfit. Arzner invests Hepburn and these pilot costumes with fetishistic power early in the film by having Hepburn play "chicken" with a male motorcyclist, running him off the road, and then appearing in this uniform to tell a roomful of rich, frivolous, fancy-dress revellers that she has never had a lover, or been married "in any sense of the word," but she is not a "prig"—just devoted to flying. This devotion to flying, she adds before striding out of the party, is the reason she keeps herself fit.

As these scenes are our introduction to Hepburn's Cynthia, Arzner is careful to set the difference marked by Cynthia's striking looks and equally striking attitudes in approving contrast to the weakness and self-indulgence of those (straights?) around her. The other out-of-place character at this party is Colin Clive's Christopher Strong (Arzner's identification figure), who is presented by his daughter to the partygoers as that rare husband who has been sexually faithful throughout a long marriage. Given this introduction, Christopher's

subsequent affair with Cynthia can be read queerly as critiquing traditional straight unions in marriage, based as they are on myths of
sexual monogamy. For Mayne, the "critical attitude toward heterosexuality" in this film

> takes the form of inflections, of bits and pieces of tone and gesture
> and emphasis, as a result of which the conventions of heterosexual
> behavior become loosened up, shaken free of some of their
> identifications with the patriarchal status quo.[23]

"Most important perhaps," Mayne continues, "the acquisition of heterosexuality becomes the downfall of Cynthia Darrington."[24]

One of the most dramatic signs of this downfall is found in the second queerly memorable Hepburn image in the film, which also pivots
around a costume and Hepburn's physical fitness. About to leave for
a party, Cynthia is delayed by Christopher, anxious to discuss his
daughter. Cynthia suddenly appears before him, and before us, as a
shimmering apparition, clad from head to toe in a remarkable form-
fitting silver lamé moth costume, which codes Hepburn as at once a
straight female spectacle, an androgynous erotic spectacle, a femme
erotic spectacle, and a camp spectacle, as she sports an elaborate
cape and curly wire antennae. Although making a dramatic, self-con-
fident entrance from her bedroom, Hepburn's Cynthia tells gay actor
Colin Clive's Christopher that she feels a little silly in the costume. A
bit later, she rebuffs his confused and tentative attempts at lovemak-
ing by telling him no one (read: no man) has ever made love to her,
and no one ever will; adding "I'm not attractive that way." Like the
proverbial moth to a flame, however, Cynthia is soon in the throes of
a torturous affair with Christopher.

From my informal interviews of lesbians and gays who have seen
Christopher Strong, it appears lesbians remember the film most vividly in terms of Hepburn running around and flying in those pilot's
outfits. Their cultural identities and erotic energies became so deeply
invested in the fetishized spectacle of a butch Hepburn in her uniform
that most lesbians I talked to completely forgot the moth costume, or
felt it represented Cynthia/Hepburn compromising her identity by
heterosexually feminizing it. Not so most gay men (including George
Cukor), who eagerly describe the sparkle of the lamé, the cling of the
fabric, the long slit that reveals Hepburn's legs as she sits, the cape,
and particularly the silver helmet with antennae that covers Hepburn's hair, allowing a certain boyish androgyny to surface in close-
ups. Of course, shots of Hepburn in the cockpit with her leather fly-

er's helmet can also have the same erotically androgynizing impact for any queerly positioned spectator. In any case, between the spectacle of butch pilot and the spectacle of androgynous moth, Arzner and Hepburn create spaces in *Christopher Strong* for the expression of queer erotics. Beyond this, these queer spaces often occur within suggestively ambiguous narrative contexts, confusing and challenging the articulation of the film's straight ideological points regarding sexuality, gender, love, and marriage.

Arzner's comment about identifying with Christopher Strong makes sapphic sense: of course she would place herself in the position of Hepburn's lover in the film. But, as Mayne points out, some of Arzner's lesbian agenda in the film is conveyed through Hepburn's dress and demeanor, which "strongly denotes lesbian identity," then and now.[25] The director's expression of this "split" lesbian identification—through a man, through a butch woman—within and underneath the terms of *Christopher Strong*'s conventional melodrama narrative is made possible because the terms here are already concerned with sympathetically depicting transgressive, convention-defying passions (whether for flying or in adultery). In fact, Arzner's queer manipulations of melodrama throughout her oeuvre would make the basis for an interesting critique combining queer auteurism and queer genre studies.[26]

Arzner's *Dance, Girl, Dance* has been the subject of straight feminist analyses, but what's here for queers?[27] Some aspects of potential queer pleasure overlap with straight feminist pleasure: for example, having women at the center not only of the narrative but of the narrative action, becoming as much agents-subjects as they are spectacularized objects. The men in this film can't quite get a purchase on the narrative. Just when it seems as if one of them will begin to control the action, Arzner narratively neutralizes them, and Maureen O'Hara's Judy, Lucille Ball's Bubbles, Maria Ouspenskaya's Madame Basilova, or Katharine Alexander's Miss Olmstead ("Olmie") steps in to move the plot along. And the narrative often moves along in terms of these women's work and their relationships to each other through their work. Mayne suggests that "female authorship acquires its most significant contours in Arzner's work through relations between and among women," and that this includes establishing a "female gaze [that] is defined early on in [*Dance, Girl, Dance*] as central to the aspirations of the women as they are shaped within a community of women."[28]

At first glance, the burlesque performer Bubbles seems to be a conventional straight golddigger who is the romantic opposition to bal-let-dancing Judy for rich alcoholic Jimmie Harris (Louis Hayward). But look again: Bubbles is jealous of Judy not primarily or ultimately because of jealousy about Jimmie. Bubbles enviously admires Judy's dancing talent, her "classiness," and her quiet strength of character. After she becomes a successful burlesque queen called "Tiger Lily White," Bubbles finds Judy and offers her a job as her lead-in act. Of course, Bubbles knows Judy's ballet dancing will be mocked by the crowd. And we know Bubbles herself will derive some satisfaction from Judy's humiliation, but not so much because Bubbles is mean-spirited as because she hopes it will place Judy on the same personal and professional level as her.

And this is just the queer point — not only is most of Bubbles's jeal-ous energy directed toward Judy, it is ultimately about Judy, in the sense that it is about Bubbles's envious admiration of Judy. She wants Judy with her, and she wants Judy in a situation she controls. Indeed, a lesbian/queer reading of *Dance, Girl, Dance* would recognize the obvious: the most compelling emotional energies and tensions develop around Bubbles's and Judy's intertwined professional and personal lives. Arzner (and Bubbles) uses Jimmie in the narrative in the same way women characters are traditionally used in "straight" male narratives — that is, as a public vehicle for transgressive erotic ex-changes between same-sex characters.[29] Bubbles loves the money and fame her solo career brings her, but she can't forget high-class Judy, so she attempts to combine the personal with the professional by convincing her manager she needs a lead-in act, and then hiring Judy for the spot.

A reading along these lines would see Bubbles's sudden decision to trick a drunken Jimmie into marriage as her way of removing a ro-mantic and sexual threat to her partnership with Judy. This interpre-tation seems reinforced by Bubbles's attempts to provoke Judy to dis-play visible signs of jealousy about the marriage. At this point they, and we, know Bubbles doesn't really care for Jimmie, and that even Judy is more devoted to her dancing career than to him. So what would this jealousy be about if it were not an indication of lesbian (or perhaps bisexual) desire?

But Judy seems more concerned about herself and her career than she is about Bubbles, although Arzner makes Judy's spectacular show- and narrative-stopping, woman-bonding, straight man-bashing speech seem to be Judy's response to the news of Bubbles's marriage to Jimmie. Thus positioned, the speech makes one wonder a bit about the possibility of Judy's repressed queerness, especially as she implicitly defends Bubbles in her indictment of straight male sexuality as the illusory base for patriarchal empowerment: "We'd laugh too," Judy shouts out to the burlesque show audience, "only we're paid to let you sit there and roll your eyes and make your screamingly clever remarks. What's it all for? So you can go home and strut before your wives and sweethearts, and play at being the stronger sex for a minute? I'm sure they see through you, just like we do!"

However, Judy's deconstruction of the straight sex show in and out of the burlesque house (and, by extension, the movie house) also signals the end of her partnership with Bubbles. Realizing this, and incensed that Judy has ruined their act, yet perhaps also encouraged by Judy's man-bashing rhetoric, Bubbles rushes out and instigates an onstage wrestling match with Judy. Although this match can be appropriated for straight uses, as it is by the cheering men in the burlesque house, it seems less a conventional "catfight," given Arzner's narrative contextualization, than the wild, confused expression of Bubbles's thwarted and not fully conscious desire for Judy.[30]

Earlier in the film, Judy, substituting for Bubbles, auditions for a job by attempting a hula. Failing to impress the club manager with her restrained movements, it appears as if Judy and the entire troupe will continue to be jobless. Enter Bubbles, who looks at Judy, sizes up the situation, and launches into a sexually suggestive hula. Bubbles's dancing here seems designed as much to show herself off to Judy, and to impress her, as it is to impress the lecherous club manager. But a full reading of how this sequence helps to establish a space for articulating lesbian desire within or alongside positions that represent straight male desire needs to consider the part played by the character of Madame Basilova in this scene, and throughout the narrative.

Madame Basilova is a once-famous Russian ballerina who has been forced to make her living by training troupes of chorus girls for nightclub floor shows. Bubbles and Judy both work in her current troupe, but Judy is the only one with a talent for classical dance, so Madame Basilova focuses her attention on training Judy for an audition with a major ballet company. Wearing plain tailored outfits and ties, Madame Basilova offers, in appearance and narrative function, striking parallels to the many publicity pictures of Dorothy Arzner at work, usually showing her gazing intently at the more traditionally feminized actresses she is directing.[31] Basilova's name also suggests that of one of Arzner's more famous lovers—the Russian actress Nazimova, who also produced films, the most notorious of which was a 1922 version of Oscar Wilde's *Salome*.[32]

Both Basilova's work training dancers—whether classical or burlesque—and Arzner's directing Hollywood actresses in straight, patriarchal narratives are concerned with presenting women as erotic spectacles. So Basilova and Arzner find themselves in rather queer positions vis-à-vis the women they work with. The dance instructor and the film director are women whose jobs encourage them, indeed require them, to assume an erotic gaze while preparing women for public presentation. In an interview, Arzner recalled the time she visited the set of a never-completed "Tarzan-type picture" in order to discuss *Christopher Strong* with Katharine Hepburn. "She was up a tree with a leopard skin on!" the director recalled, adding, "She had a marvelous figure."[33]

In *Dance, Girl, Dance* Arzner appears to acknowledge the erotics of her own position as Hollywood film director through her treatment of Madame Basilova. Simultaneously, Arzner demonstrates how easily supposedly straight male erotic spectator positions might be claimed as sites of lesbian/queer pleasure. The scene I mentioned in which Bubbles dances the hula for Judy (and, one might add, for Madame Basilova) is one example of how a lesbian erotic gaze is negotiated in *Dance, Girl, Dance*. Even more striking is the sequence Arzner constructs around Madame Basilova's secretive and pleasurable gazing at Judy while she practices a dance.

Lured by music playing above her office, Basilova climbs the stairs. Before reaching the top, she stops and positions herself behind the balustrade, glancing off at Judy. As Basilova places herself to gaze at Judy, the camera makes a graceful tracking curve away from Basilova, positioning itself so that our first sight of Judy is clearly *not* Basilova's; it is a spectator position emphatically established as being *next to* Basilova's, which offers Judy as a (sexual, entertainment, identificatory) spectacle for those "not Basilova" viewers—straight men, by traditional feminist theoretical convention, but also, potentially, gays, bisexuals, and straight women. Subsequent shots of Judy, however, will represent Basilova's gaze in their angle and distance, until Basilova sneaks down the stairs and the shot of Judy returns to a non-point-of-view one, which now encourages a range of erotic responses from viewers, as the previous sequence has marked at least two different eroticized spectator positions in relation to the spectacle of Judy's dance.

In this sequence, by the simple expedient of making a culturally invisible spectator active and visible in her spectatorship, Arzner suggests something extraordinary: the space for queer expression has always existed within, or alongside, what traditionally have been considered straight cultural forms and conventions. These forms and conventions only seem inevitably bound to express straight positions because, historically, they have been used most often, and most visibly, to promote straight ideologies and desires. Make queer positions visible and differentiate them from straight positions, Arzner implies in *Dance, Girl, Dance*, and we can articulate queer discourses right in the heart of existing cultural forms—no secret (sub)cultural coding, recoding, and decoding necessary.

Cukor's *Camille* also contains moments where actors and the construction of the gaze work together to create queer spaces within an apparently straight narrative. A queer reading of *Camille* might begin by considering its director and its stars, Greta Garbo and Robert Taylor.[34] There is plenty of irony in recognizing that these queer talents are recreating a legendary heterosexual romance, with the help of gay actor Rex O'Malley in a major supporting role. Marguerite and Armand, the characters portrayed by the stars, are plagued by disease—she has tuberculosis, he is pathologically jealous—so their desire is marked as tainted and unhealthy. Marguerite is a courtesan whose wild living has brought on her illness, while Armand's jealous outbursts are the result of sexual possessiveness. Although Cukor and his actors wring every bit of sympathy and eroticism from the story, straight narrative conventions demand that Marguerite's and Armand's forbidden passion end as a *Liebestod*.

Adding further cultural dimensions to her role as Marguerite is Garbo's history as a queer cult favorite. These gay, lesbian, and bisexual cults prize her screen image for its strong beauty and the mystery (at least to nonqueers) of her emotional distance from most of the people and events around her—that is, from the straight narratives and characters. But, as Cukor once remarked, Garbo's screen persona was "rather cool, but seething underneath," and in *Camille* and other films, she found moments in which to establish a "rapport with an audience" by letting them "know she was thinking things, and thinking them uncensored."[35] Particularly notable in the on-screen development of this kind of rapport with queer audiences have been those moments when Garbo's acting suggests an erotically charged bond between her character and another, usually younger, female character, or a male child: in *Queen Christina*, *Love*, *Anna Karenina*, and, in *Camille*, in the relationship between Marguerite and her best friend, Nichette (Elizabeth Allan).[36]

Also queerly interesting in *Camille* is the manner in which Cukor, Garbo, and Taylor invest the straight, patriarchal narrative with a "difference" that implicitly works to deprivilege the heteroerotic, as it is ultimately set within a range of erotic choices. For example, although on display for others (including the film audience) early in the film in a box seat at the opera, Marguerite trains her opera glasses on Armand's beauty with obvious voyeuristic pleasure. His pleased recognition of her gazing moves Marguerite to speak to her companions about her attraction to him. Cukor directs Garbo and Taylor's subsequent love scenes to capitalize upon this initial, unconventional sexual power dynamic, so these scenes become fascinating moments during which viewers can experience pleasure across a wide range of erotic positions—particularly in the scene where a seated Taylor passively receives kisses all over his face from a standing Garbo, who keeps her arms extended down by her sides. Of Garbo and this scene, Cukor remarked:

> I find that people who leave their mark are bold and uncensored in the way they think. . . . Now, for example in *Camille* there was a scene where Armand left a party—the most extraordinary erotic and titillating scene. Garbo had her hands at her sides, and she kissed Armand on his face, all over; and it generated the most extraordinary eroticism. And that's because she was thinking certain things; and that's what did it—thinking boldly and without fear and without censorship.[37]

Here and elsewhere, Cukor's almost excessive repetition of "uncensored" and "eroticism" together suggests that there may be more to the sexual dynamics of *Camille* and certain of his other films than their straight narratives overtly proclaim. Surely it is not heterosexual eroticism that is being censored in a film such as *Camille*.

And what of this eroticism that dare not speak its name? I—and thousands of queers—used to cry at the end of *Camille* because of a shifting masochistic identification with both Marguerite's ecstatic death-in-love and the beginnings of Armand's necrophiliac erotic obsession. In either case, not very empowering tears of romanticized self-pity were shed over what queers on- and offscreen supposed was the inevitably tragic fate of "sick" and forbidden desires.[38] Now, years later, my tears at the end of *Camille* represent remnants of nostalgic, regressive self-pity mixed with a sad sense that Garbo, Taylor, and Cukor are pantomiming individual and cultural tragedies, depicting the impossibility of directly expressing the queer desire they all felt, in a film they clearly cared so much about. Garbo's/Marguerite's last words to Taylor/Armand allude to the pathos of the film's closeted ethos: "Perhaps it is better if I live in your heart, where the world can't see me. If I'm dead, there will be no stain on our love."

But all is not pathos in possible queer readings of *Camille*. There is actually one queer-positive secondary character, perhaps two. The one I'm certain of is Rex O'Malley's Gaston, who supports transgressive desire by acting as a go-between for Marguerite and Armand — when he's not seeing drunken, middle-aged ex-courtesans safely home, that is, or accompanying them to the opera or to auctions. After all her straight friends have deserted her, Gaston remains to help care for Marguerite during her final illness, prompting her admission, "I used to think you were a gay fellow with no other thought but pleasure." In Gaston, Cukor and O'Malley created a character without precedent in Hollywood films to that time: a sympathetic feminine gay man who goes to parties, gossips, and is vain about his looks and clothes, while also being concerned about the well-being of other people.[39] This sympathetic treatment is extended to none of the non-queer supporting characters in the film. The second possible queer-positive character in *Camille* is Nanine, Marguerite's loyal, gruffly concerned, and motherly personal maid. Like Gaston, Nanine encourages Marguerite's class- and age-defying relationship with Armand, forming an alliance with Gaston to care for Marguerite, as well as to effect a reunion between the transgressive lovers.

While *Camille*'s characters and narrative remain in the realm of queer suggestiveness and connotation, Cukor's *Sylvia Scarlett*, made a year earlier, is one of the queerest films ever made in Hollywood. This is the film in which Katharine Hepburn plays a teenaged boy for most of the running time. It opens with a printed prologue that hints at the queerness to come: "To the adventurer, to all who stray from the beaten track, life is an extravagance in which laughter and luck and love come in odd ways; but they are nonetheless sweet for that." Cukor had wanted the film to begin with Hepburn already dressed as a boy, but the studio forced him to modify this opening: "We had to add a silly, frivolous prologue, to explain *why* this girl was dressed like a boy, and being so good at it. We weren't allowed to give the impression that she liked it, or that she's done it before, or that it came naturally."[40]

Although a commercial failure in 1936, many critics were taken with Hepburn's abilities as androgyne. *Time* magazine's critic noted the film revealed "the interesting fact that Katharine Hepburn is better-looking as a boy than as a woman." The *New York Herald Tribune* effused, "The dynamic Miss Hepburn is the handsomest boy of the season."[41] Discussing *Sylvia Scarlett* in his first book on cult films, Danny Peary finds it "quite remarkable that during a period when such things as transvestism and bisexuality were taboo no one even mentioned the strange sights found in this picture."[42] Peary proceeds to enumerate some of these "strange sights" in language that veers between the heterocentric and the homophobic. "We actually see Katharine Hepburn kissed on the lips by another woman," Peary breathlessly notes. And he feels compelled to follow this observation with the straight-comforting explanation that this queer kiss occurs "when Maudie thinks Sylvia is a boy and tries to seduce 'him.' "[43]

Peary then goes on about the scene in which the artist Michael Fane invites the person he knows as Sylvester to share a bed with him. Though Peary tries to suggest that "Fane's intentions may be innocent," he adds, "but how many men in their thirties are such good friends with teen-aged boys?"[44] "Then, of course," Peary concludes, "there is Fane's famous line to 'Sylvester': 'I don't know what it is that gives me a queer feeling when I look at you.' "[45] Actually Peary misquotes the line. What Fane says to Sylvester is "I know [not 'I don't know'] what it is that gives me a queer feeling when I look at you." Peary's rewriting bespeaks denial and repression of queerness; Cukor's film of the recognition and assertion of queerness. And it is a queerness that ultimately has bisexuality as the foundation of its erotic politics: Michael Fane, the painter (Brian Aherne); Jimmy Monkley, the con artist (Cary Grant); and Lily, the countess (Natalie Paley) are all shown to be attracted both to Sylvester and to Sylvia. Since we know Sylvester is Sylvia, even Maudie's (Dennie Moore) flirtations with Sylvester carry some bisexual charge in addition to their lesbian suggestiveness. The narrative concludes with the union of two bisexual couples: Jimmy and Lily (after she leaves Fane) and Fane and Sylvia-Sylvester.

The public and critical silence in 1936 about the "strange sights" in *Sylvia Scarlett* is not so remarkable considering that a commentator in 1981 can't even see what the film is really about—or, perhaps, can't comfortably accept what he sees because it gives him the same "queer feelings" Fane gets when he looks at Sylvester. After homophobically declaring that "modern thinking has added unfortunate connotations" to "trans-gender impersonation," Cukor critic Gary Carey admits that audiences who find cross-gender material "embarrassing and alienating" do so because "too often it cuts close to our own suspicions about the actors involved or to our fears about ourselves."[46]

Queerly seen, *Sylvia Scarlett* is an erotically daring film whose seriocomic uses of transvestism within the conventions of a mistaken identity plot playfully invite all spectators to experience "queer feelings" as they move through the range of homo-, bi-, and heterosexual desires articulated in the text. And the film gains added dimensions if you know that Cary Grant's real-life bisexuality could be playing a major role in its gender- and sexuality-blurring proceedings. While Cukor and Hepburn often joked about the film as a failure, Cukor said he was pleased about its "sexuality before its time" cult status, admitting that although *Sylvia Scarlett* was "a flop" it was "still [his] favorite picture."[47] No doubt much of Cukor's fondness for the film had to do with what he called the "impertinence" of the project, and his collaboration with Hepburn, Grant, and scenarist John Collier ("a daring kind of writer").[48] "But the picture did something to me," Cukor told one interviewer. "It slowed me up. I wasn't going to be so goddamned daring after that. I thought, 'Well, kiddo, don't you break all sorts of new paths, you just watch it.' "[49]

Three years before *Sylvia Scarlett*, Hepburn revealed her butch potential for the first time in film as record-breaking pilot Cynthia Darrington in Arzner's *Christopher Strong* and as Jo March in Cukor's *Little Women*, in which she cut off her hair to raise money for her mother. A queer-cultural-history-meets-auteurism question occurs here: Would Hepburn's screen image have been established as quite so appealingly butch, or androgynous if you like, if Cukor and Arzner hadn't been assigned to guide her through most of her early RKO star-making films, including her screen debut in Cukor's *A Bill of Divorcement* (1932)? In the context of queer film history, it is no coincidence that Hepburn's best post-1930s butch role was in Cukor's *Pat and Mike*, in which she plays a professional athlete.[50]

Arzner's and Cukor's important connection to a star image that has been developed in queer cultures largely without reference to directorial auteurism brings this essay back to its original question about authorship, queerness, and queer cultures. That is, how compatible are auteurist cult-of-the-director (star, writer, etc.) notions with non-academic and academic queer approaches to mass culture?

Armed with the knowledge of Cukor's and Arzner's queerness (even if we can't always be certain about how they would define it), and knowing of their often highly influential roles in production, we might recognize a queer version of authorship in which queerly positioned readers examine mass culture texts—here Cukor and Arzner films—in order to indicate where and how the queer discourses of both producers and readers might be articulated within, alongside, or against the presumably straight ideological agendas of most texts. These types of queer readings are tricky and interesting because they establish queer authorial discourses by negotiating a range of textual meanings caught somewhere between auteurist considerations of director (or star, writer, etc.) intentionality and cultural / cultural studies considerations of reception practices and uses of texts. Most generally, I hope this chapter has suggested the potential for combining queer cultural history and cultural practices with established critical and theoretical models, such as auteurism and authorship, in order to develop a variety of distinctively queer-inflected approaches to discussing mass culture.

CHAPTER THREE

I Love Laverne and Shirley:

Lesbian Narratives, Queer Pleasures, and Television Sitcoms

66 A t Last! Lost Memoirs of 'Lucy' Costar: 'Ethel' Tells
All—Even Truth About Rumors She and Lucy
Were Lesbian Lovers" screams the front-page headline of the August
29, 1989, *National Enquirer*. The story inside features pictures of
Vivian Vance and Lucille Ball together offscreen and in their *I Love
Lucy* roles as Ethel Mertz and Lucy Ricardo, as well as the first in-
stallment of excerpts from Vance's "explosive secret autobiography,"
which begins:

> Lucille Ball and I were just like sisters. We adored each other's
> company. She and I had so many laughs on "I Love Lucy" that we
> could hardly get through filming without cracking up.
>   Then I began hearing that Lucille and I were too close.
>   My first husband disapproved of my closeness with Lucille. "People
> are talking about you two," he'd say. "You ought to be careful about
> the hugging and kissing you do on the show."
>   The word in Pacific Palisades, where I lived, was that something
> was wrong with me, something my analyst wouldn't tell me about.[1]

This story of straight male hysteria breeding misogyny and homophobia in order to undermine close bonds between women is de-
pressingly familiar. What is particularly interesting in this case is
how the relations between actual women (Ball and Vance) are mixed
and conflated with those of two fictional characters (Lucy and Ethel)
to create a narrative of lesbian desire. This lesbian narrative is constructed by male homophobes here: the husband, the analyst, and
Vance's second husband's best friend, who found the autobiography,
and reports that this second husband told him "the hardest thing for
Vivian to write about was the Hollywood rumors that she and Lucy   *39*

had a lesbian relationship, but that she wanted to set the record straight."[2]

While Vance seems worried about the rumors, she also seems to consider lesbian desire a possible explanation of her feelings for Ball. When she begins to hear the gossip about herself and Ball, Vance visits her analyst to ask him, "Is there anything the matter with me that you've never told me?" After recording her analyst's assurances that she is fine, Vance puts aside the lesbian narrative in its patriarchal, homophobic form, only to pick it up immediately in another:

> Lucille and I used to watch our own shows and rock with laughter at what we'd done on camera. We thought we were knockouts in some routines.
>
> Before shooting, Lucille and I would do advance planning. We'd plot together: "What if I step on your head when I climb down from the upper berth? . . . Suppose we both get so busy crawling around on the floor that we back into each other under the table? . . .
>
> But throughout the "Lucy" years I was in analysis, trying to sort out crossed wires in my life.
>
> I was married to a man, an actor, who liked to dominate and discipline me. I kept trying to please him, but nothing I did was right. There were times when I would literally beat my head against the bedroom wall in frustration. . . .
>
> Analysis finally helped me. And working with Lucille Ball, seeing all the strength she had, was good and healthy for me.[3]

Ultimately Vance also conflates herself and her feelings for Ball with her performance of Ethel and Ethel's relationship with Lucy. But this contra-heterosexual, women-bonding narrative—this lesbian narrative—is cast in positive terms, finding its happy ending in the work, friendship, and love between two women.[4]

The ways in which Vance's and Ball's offscreen lives have been discussed in relation to their roles as Ethel and Lucy in order to express various discourses of lesbianism provide the background for analyzing other situation comedies in which the relationships between women are the *raisons d'être* of the series. It is no coincidence that the public and the press are concerned about monitoring on-the-set relationships as well as those offscreen between the main actors on these series, or that this news/gossip often influences how characters and narratives (individual episode narratives as well as a series' meganarrative) are read. Robert H. Deming, in "*Kate and Allie*: 'New Women' and the Audience's Television Archive," speaks briefly about how some of the "media discourses" surrounding these series "gave female characters a life-like dimension outside of the text," listing *TV Guide* articles such as "I'd Walk Through a Dark Alley with Cagney and Lacey Behind Me," "No Jiggles. No Scheming. Just Real Women as Friends," and "Are *Kate and Allie* Such Good Friends — Off Screen?" as examples.[5] Then there has been the extensively reported on-the-set feuding between Cindy Williams (Shirley) and Penny Marshall (Laverne), and, more recently, the estrangement of Delta Burke (Suzanne Sugarbaker) from her costars and from producer-writer Linda Bloodworth-Thomason on *Designing Women*.[6]

As these examples indicate, media and public interest in women-centered series is focused upon potential dissension among the actors. It is almost as if mass audience pleasure week after week in seeing pairs and groups of women characters in intense and enjoyable relationships must be tempered or undermined somehow by news about how the women who play these characters have problems with each other. These misogynistic and, I would contend, homophobic public discursive and media tactics are nothing new, of course. There were constant radio, newspaper, and magazine reports about the production of George Cukor's 1939 film *The Women*, depicting the filming as fraught with the jealousy and temperament of a cast of 135 women — and one "women's director." This type of publicity was featured at the time and has been quoted in relation to the production of the film ever since, even though Cukor repeatedly stated that all the actors behaved professionally, and they formed a "rather jolly bunch."[7]

Considering the interests of patriarchal heterosexual culture, it is not surprising most of its media should want to devalue any potential site of woman-centered pleasures in mass culture, particularly when these pleasures fundamentally rely on viewers assuming queer positions. What is so interesting about series such as *I Love Lucy* (and, later, *The Lucy Show*), *Laverne and Shirley*, *Designing Women*, *The Golden Girls*, *Babes*, *227*, *The Mary Tyler Moore Show*, *Kate and Allie*, and *Alice* is their crucial investment in constructing narratives that connect an audience's pleasure to the activities and relationships of women — which results in situating most male characters as potential threats to the spectator's narrative pleasure.[8] It is this kind of narrative construction I am calling "lesbian." The spectator positions and pleasures audiences take in relation to these lesbian sitcoms I call either "lesbian" (for self-identified lesbians) or "queer" (for anybody else).

The ideas behind Adrienne Rich's term "lesbian continuum" work well here, as this concept suggests that a wide range and degree of experience and emotion might be called "lesbian":

> I mean the term *lesbian continuum* to include a range . . . of woman-
> identified experience; not simply the fact that a woman has had or
> consciously desired genital sexual experience with another woman.
> If we expand it to embrace many more forms of primary intensity
> between and among women, including the sharing of a rich inner life,
> the bonding against male tyranny, the giving and receiving of practical
> and political support . . . we begin to grasp breadths of female history
> and psychology that have lain out of reach as a consequence of
> limited, mostly clinical, definitions of "lesbianism."[9]

In separating the concept of a lesbian continuum from Rich's notion of "lesbian existence" as the material, historical presence of lesbians and their "continuing creation of the meaning of [lesbian] existence,"[10] I believe I am not taking anything away from the expressions of specifically lesbian cultures and identities. What I am suggesting here is that in mass culture reception, at least, the idea of a lesbian continuum might be adapted and expanded to include those situations in which anyone identifies with or takes pleasure in the "many . . . forms of primary intensity between and among women" elaborated in shows such as *Laverne and Shirley*, *The Mary Tyler Moore Show*, and *Designing Women*.

Within these terms, you don't need to be lesbian-identified to respond to the lesbian elements of narrative construction in these sitcoms. My approach in the following pages is not so much concerned with ways of reading and taking pleasure in these shows *as* a lesbian, but rather ways of queerly reading *with*, and taking queer pleasure *in*, the lesbian tenor or temper of these series. This approach does include specifically lesbian positions and pleasures insofar as self-identified lesbians share the readings I offer of these shows.[11]

As with spectators, so with the women characters in these sitcoms. The fundamentally lesbian foundations of narrative construction in these shows don't mean that the major characters need necessarily be read as subtextual or closeted lesbians. As Marilyn R. Farwell points out, borrowing "from Teresa de Lauretis's distinction between character and narrative space we can conclude that a lesbian [character] can occupy heterosexual space and a heterosexual can occupy . . . lesbian narrative space."[12] I am more concerned in this section with how various lesbian narrative structures and spectator positions are developed and expressed in certain television situation comedies than in identifying isolated subtextual or queer cult lesbian characters or star personas (such as Sally Rogers/Rose Marie on *The Dick Van Dyke Show*, Alice/Ann B. Davis on *The Brady Bunch*, and Aunt Bea/ Frances Bavier on *The Andy Griffith Show*).

However, since the sitcoms I discuss do present heterosexually marked characters in lesbian-charged spaces, they also allow for, and even encourage, readings of most of the women characters as "really" lesbian for viewers who use something like Rich's continuum to define "lesbian." My allegiance to the concepts of queerness and Rich's lesbian continuum in relation to understanding narrative construction and reception practices dispose me to read the dynamics between most of the women characters in the series mentioned in this section as lesbian in some way. From where I sit as a feminine gay, I will often see fundamentally lesbian bonding where others see straight homosocial bonding, or, perhaps, a homosocial bonding that jokingly plays with suggestions of lesbian desire.

Most frequently sitcoms such as *The Golden Girls*, *Kate and Allie*, and *Designing Women* point toward lesbian readings through double entendres; oblique, displaced, or jokey references to lesbianism; or with "lesbian episodes." These "lesbian episodes" are those individual shows that feature characters clearly marked as "lesbian" in them, and whose project it is to raise, and then to contain or deflect, the lesbian charge—or the charge of lesbianism—the series has accumulated around its regular cast. Typically, these epsiodes encourage playful and comic connections between the "real" lesbians and the other women in the cast through jokes, double entendres, and cases of mistaken identity or misassumption. Yet these episodes are also particularly insistent about maintaining the idea of homosociality ("just friends") as fully distinct and apart from (as well as preferable to) the homosexual through another network of jokes that work to contain, disempower, or devalue visible representations of lesbianism.

Mimi White effectively summarizes the complex intersection of queer readers/queer cultures and women-centered sitcoms:

> Programs such as *The Golden Girls* and *Kate and Allie* offer the narrative premise of adult women living together as a family. The female characters in these shows—in couples or in groups—are firmly established as heterosexual, and episodes regularly deal with dating, the desire for male companionship, and past marriages. But at the same time, they validate women's bonding as a form of social stability, a viable and attractive alternative to the traditional family, and even

hint at the possibility of lesbian lifestyles—at least as far as possible
within dominant ideology. A subcultural reading would emphasize
these aspects of the program. . . . Indeed, such a reading might stress
that on a week-to-week basis the narrative privileges women's relations
over their inadequate, transient dealings with men.[13]

The one point on which I would differ with White is her categorizing
such readings as always *sub*cultural, alternative, or "reading against
the grain"—they are particular queer cultural readings of mass culture texts. Besides, as I have suggested, reading and enjoying mass
culture texts such as *The Golden Girls* queerly in one way or another
can be, and is, done by audiences of all sexual identities.[14] Indeed,
the sitcoms I am concerned with encourage, and in many ways position, audiences to read and enjoy queerly, whether they would call it
this or not. Specifically, they are positioned to take lesbian or queer
pleasures in the development of women's relationships within situation comedy narratives.

But, as suggested earlier, this type of lesbian narrative construction and its attendant queer pleasures are not without their potential
ideological problems. It is possible to see these sitcoms as performing
certain homophobic cultural work as they construct and encourage
pleasures that seek to have fundamentally lesbian narratives and en-
joyments pass as straight or as "just friends" homosocial. With the
surfaces of their characters, actions, and mise-en-scène insistently
straight-coded, these sitcoms are allowed to present a wide range of
intense women-bonding that straight audiences can safely enjoy because the codes of lesbian "femme-ininity" can also be read as representing the straight feminine. Christine Holmlund discusses this exploitation of the representational codes of femme-ininity in order to
"sort of" treat lesbianism in films such as *Entre Nous* and *Personal
Best*: "The unconscious deployment . . . of a cinematic lesbian continuum organized around the figure of the femme is politically and
erotically ambiguous, both presenting and erasing lesbian identities
and sexualities."[15] In relation to modern advertising, Danae Clark
has also noted that "the sexual indeterminacy" found in attempts to
target straights and lesbians simultaneously "allows a space for lesbian identification, but must necessarily deny the representation of
lesbian identity politics."[16]

Clearly, the sitcoms I will discuss in this section do everything they
can to assert a homosocial, "just friends" understanding of both the
narrative camaraderie between their femme-inine characters and the

audience's pleasure in this sight. As an April 1992 *TV Guide* ad promoting *Room for Two* (about a mother and daughter who work together) and *Sibs* (about three sisters) exclaims: "Grab Your Popcorn . . . It's a solid hour of *female* bonding!" But besides the (overly) insistent italicizing of "female" and the exclamation point, the ad offers a quote from the *Cleveland Plain Dealer* about *Sibs* that suggests another way of describing and understanding the appeal of these women-centered shows as "witty, sexy, adult" programs.[17] The project of the following analyses of *I Love Lucy*, *The Mary Tyler Moore Show*, *Laverne and Shirley*, and *Designing Women* is to discuss their "adult, sexy, witty" narratives and pleasures as fundamentally lesbian or queer, while acknowledging that my understanding and use of the term "lesbian" in relation to these narratives and characters works within the same broad definition that these very shows — like the films and advertising Holmlund and Clark critique — employ to simultaneously suggest and deny culturally and erotically specific forms of lesbianism. In the face of all this, I still maintain that these sitcoms' basic structuring principle can be called lesbian, even if these shows often seem to offer only hypothetically lesbian surfaces that encourage closeted queer enjoyment.[18]

One episode of *Kate and Allie* cleverly acknowledges the show's lesbian situation-comedy lineage when Allie falls asleep on the sofa and dreams that she and Kate are Lucy Ricardo and Ethel Mertz, and then Mary Richards and Rhoda Morgenstern. As the material at the beginning of this section implies, at some point in the run of *I Love Lucy* (1951–57), people began to read the closeness between Lucy and Ethel as encompassing the erotic. Recognizing that these erotics were the center of *I Love Lucy*'s narrative pleasures was not so clear during the show's initial run, perhaps, as it is in retrospect with the evidence of *The Lucy Show* (1962–68) and *Here's Lucy* (1968–74).[19] *The Lucy Show* was initially built around Lucille Carmichael (Lucille Ball) and Vivian Bagley (Vivian Vance), a widow and a divorcée living together with their children.[20] When Vance left the show, Ball recruited Ann Sothern, Joan Blondell, and Mary Jane Crofts to play her cohort for extended periods. The first *Lucy Show* after Vance's departure has a butched-up Lucy (in a grey suit and string tie) reading a letter from the just-married "Viv" who says the best thing about her marriage to a Mr. Burnside is that she won't have to change the initials on her luggage.

Looking back at *I Love Lucy*, the strength and dynamism of Lucy and Ethel's relationship are simultaneously the most consistent source of the show's pleasures and the source of the greatest threats to the narrative's maintaining some form of patriarchal heterosexual hegemony. While as a couple Lucy and Ethel only achieve partial or temporary disruptions of the status quo, the series depends on their lesbian comic energies to establish and propel most *I Love Lucy* narratives, thus encouraging a number of fascinating scenes and episodes during the show's long run. In "Vacation from Marriage" (October 27, 1952), the Ricardos and the Mertzes split up into same-sex couples after Lucy and Ethel decide their heterosexual relationships with Ricky and Fred are in "a rut." In an attempt to make their husbands envious, the women appear at the Ricardos' apartment (where the men are staying) dressed to go out nightclubbing. "I hope you two will have as gay an evening as we are," Lucy says to Ricky and Fred. But instead of going to the 21 Club, Lucy and Ethel return to the Mertzes' bedroom, where they have the following exchange:

LUCY: How do you like it here at 21?

ETHEL: *Très* gay.

Although the narrative motivation for all this is the women's attempts to get the men to call off the "vacation from marriage," the ultimate "gayness" of the show's female same-sex comradeship is established here as overtly as it ever can or will be.

In a more connotative or associative register, moments such as Lucy's imitating Tallulah Bankhead's gender-transgressing deep voice or her cross-dressing masculine or butch, and her butch-femme role-playing with Ethel (as reporters, as a male-female vaudeville team, Lucy as the writer-director of an operetta in which Ethel is the soprano star, as cowboys in a homemade Western film, Lucy as a baseball player) often work to reinforce those fundamental queer pleasures in the narrative for certain viewers by evoking lesbian cultural codes and references. Of Lucy and Ethel's comic teamwork, Patricia Mellencamp notes that its "reliance on physical comedy rather than verbal comedy, with Lucy and Ethel as the lead performers, constituted another exclusion of Ricky."[21]

One of the most interesting episodes along these lines is "Lucy Is Envious" (March 29, 1954), in which Lucy and Ethel earn money by taking a stunt job publicizing the film *Women from Mars*. In their androgynizing Martian uniforms, Lucy and Ethel appear atop King Kong's phallic realm, the Empire State Building, and terrorize a group of tourists, as much by the strange language the pair have made up as by their looks. Frightened when a straight Earth woman screams after Lucy peers into her mouth, the alien women use their "paralyzing ray" to silence one of the men (the stunt's promoter), who threatens to warn the world. The stunt over, but still in their costumes, Lucy and Ethel return home. Joyfully leaping about as they count their wages, the women continue to speak to each other in "Martian." With their androgynous look and their incomprehensible language, Lucy and Ethel's difference is coded as dangerous and alien. Since they are set apart from straight Earth men and women here, there is little doubt as to what this difference is really all about. The sight (and sound) of Lucy and Ethel returning home as Martian women is so startling and weirdly funny that the rest of the episode's narrative works to completely reverse what has come before by having Ricky and Fred play men from Mars in order to scare "the girls" back into their roles as submissive housewives.

Integrating Lucille Ball's pregnancy into *I Love Lucy*'s text established a precedent, and a pattern, for having women-centered sitcoms use expectant motherhood to reinforce and expand the women-bonding aspects of their narratives. Far from shifting the series's emphasis toward heterosexual domestic concerns, as might be expected, the pregnancy and postpartum episodes of *I Love Lucy, Laverne and Shirley, Designing Women, The Golden Girls, The Mothers-in-Law,* and *Bewitched* are concerned with marginalizing and trivializing male characters while (re)establishing a network of supportive women around the mother(-to-be).[22] The famous "Lucy is Enciente" episode (October 12, 1952) opens with Lucy and Ethel recalling their grandmothers, after which Ethel suggests Lucy's "dauncy" feeling might be a sign of pregnancy. Returning from the doctor's office, Lucy turns to Ethel in a blissful daze: "Ethel, we're going to have a baby." "We are?" Ethel exclaims, "Oh, isn't that wonderful, I never had a baby before." "You knew it even before I did," Lucy responds, adding, "This whole thing was practically your idea." In contrast, Lucy finds it nearly impossible to tell Ricky about her pregnancy—indeed, the episode is constructed so that he tells himself while a silent Lucy nods her assent. The episodes that follow this one would be good illustrations of feminist cultural and psychoanalytic theories about how motherhood establishes erotic bonds between women, including mothers and daughters.[23] Lucy's maternity, from being narratively conceived, in a manner of speaking, between her and Ethel, is developed to bring Lucy's mother (Mrs. McGillicuddy) and the upstairs neighbor/ babysitter (Mrs. Trumbell) into the series as regulars to form a strong community of women. Besides this, these epsiodes remind us that there have always been strong mother-daughter elements in Ethel and Lucy's relationship, with Lucy the childish one who occasionally makes joking references to Ethel as a mother figure for her (as in "Lucy Writes a Novel," May 4, 1954).

The Mary Tyler Moore Show (1970–77) also worked out some of its lesbian narratives through the matrix of motherhood and mother-daughter relations. As if to indicate that the interactions among the women characters in the ensemble cast were the heart of the show's narrative appeal, only Mary Richards (Mary Tyler Moore) and her best friend Rhoda Morgenstern (Valerie Harper) were given mothers who were recurring characters (played by Nanette Fabray and Nancy Walker). Phyllis Lindstrom (Cloris Leachman), their landlady, is the mother of Bess, who in one episode leaves Phyllis and "adopts" Mary as her new mother. Another episode has Phyllis ask Mary to tell Bess all about sex. In addition, Mary's Aunt Flo (Eileen Heckart) makes a number of memorable appearances in which she outtalks and out-drinks Mary's gruff boss, Lou Grant. Fathers (Mary's, Rhoda's, Ted's) do appear on a number of episodes, but they are almost always narratively less important than mothers and mother-daughter pairs. Besides, the women are given most of the funniest lines and situations.[24]

Of course, local television news producer Lou Grant (who also functioned as a father figure for Mary), head writer Murray Slaughter, and newscaster Ted Baxter do have their moments, as well as having entire shows built around them.[25] But many of the episodes ostensibly focused on Lou are concerned with his divorce or his dating, and both situations bring new women characters onto the show, or involve established characters such as Aunt Flo, "Happy Homemaker" Sue Ann Nivens, and even Mary and Rhoda. As far as Ted and Murray are concerned, for a number of seasons many viewers (consciously or not) considered them gay or bisexual—or, in the words of Richard Corliss, audiences had "suspected" them of being "closet queens."[26] Viewers often read as effeminate, and therefore as gay, such things as Ted's overweening vanity about his looks and Murray's bitchy *bon mot* dialogue, which is usually directed at Ted in a tone of mixed irritation and affection. Thus (ef)feminized, Ted and Murray narratively become two more of "the girls," particularly when counterpoised with Lou, Gordy the weatherman, or one of Mary's dates.[27] Perhaps sensing these readings of Murray and Ted, the show's producers and writers made a concerted effort to heterosexualize the two men around the third season by bringing on Murray's wife as a recurring character and introducing Georgette Franklin (Georgia Engel) as Ted's girlfriend and later his wife.

But Georgette's addition to the cast in the middle of the show's third season, followed by that of Sue Ann Nivens (Betty White) at the beginning of the fourth season, was also a conscious effort by the show's creators to "build a second generation of supporting players . . . to keep the series strong over the long haul."[28] With Harper's departure at the end of the fourth season and Leachman's during the fifth (both to star in spin-off series named after their characters), Georgette and Sue Ann were developed as major characters to replace Rhoda and Phyllis.[29] However, with Rhoda and Phyllis (and Mrs. Morgenstern) gone, the show's last two seasons lost those all-women narratives about Mary's life at home. Her move from the old apartment building she shared with Rhoda, Bess, and Phyllis to an ultramodern apartment signaled the program's switch from lesbian narratives to more heterosexual(ized) ones.

Typical plots began to revolve around Ted and Georgette's marriage, their adoption of a boy genius, Mary's dates, her new steady boyfriend (played by *That Girl* beau Ted Bessell), Lou's dates, his relationship with Mary's aunt Flo, and Sue Ann's attempts to get Lou into bed. Indeed, the last two seasons become positively incestuous in their heterosexual plotting, with episodes in which Murray falls in love with Mary; Lou goes on a date with Mary; Mary dates Murray's father; Lou dates (and proposes to) Mary's aunt; and Lou, Murray, and Ted dream what it would be like to be married to Mary. Only occasionally does the series attempt a return to the lesbian narratives that had made the show popular, as with episodes featuring Aunt Flo or Sue Ann's sister, or the one in which Georgette gives birth in Mary's apartment, with Sue Ann and Mary assisting. One indication of just how invested viewers were in the queer pleasures of the show's initial women-centered narratives is the series's precipitous slip in the Neilsen ratings to nineteenth and then to thirty-ninth place in its last two seasons after being ranked between seventh and eleventh place during the previous four seasons.[30]

I will let a detailed discussion of one episode stand in for the types of lesbian narratives/queer pleasures the series generated in its prime. This episode has Phyllis and Mary both seeing the same man, Mike (John Saxon), but its title, "Ménage-à-Phyllis," suggests that the power dynamics in this erotically charged trio lie with a woman, and that, therefore, the two other partners in Phyllis's ménage are Mike and Mary. Since it contains some obvious gay references, the narrative also seems willing to present certain aspects of women's relationships in a manner just barely this side of lesbian connotation. The episode's premise is that because Lars doesn't like to go to cultural events, Phyllis asks Mike, who has just broken his engagement, to be her escort. After Mary mentions Phyllis and Mike's arrangement, Ted remarks that it is "disgusting" to hear Phyllis is "running around." When Mary explains that Phyllis and Mike only go to the ballet and opera together as friends, Ted flips his wrist limply and says, "Oh, he's one of *those*!" Defending Mike against Ted's innuendo, Mary can't even say the term Ted implies: "No! Why does everyone think that just because a man likes ballet he's . . . No! He's not!" When Mike arrives in the newsroom to speak to Mary, Ted tries to be hiply tolerant, though after Mike leaves, he turns to Murray and says, "I just hope he's not using Mary to get to me."

On a night she is supposed to go out with Mike, Phyllis comes down with a cold, and Mary visits her with some ice cream and magazines. Lying on the sofa, Phyllis nostalgically recalls how her mother used to bring her ice cream when she was a little girl, and about how she told her mother she "wuved" everything: "I wuv my ice cream," "I wuv my teddy bear," "I wuv my mommy." When Mike arrives, Phyllis insists Mary take her place at the opera but asks her to bring back something—Mike. With Mary as the "mommy" as well as the rival for a man's affection, the show seems to be working itself out in straight "Electra complex" terms at this point, but the episode's second half moves the material firmly into the realm of lesbian narrative/queer pleasure by methodically downgrading, reducing, and eliminating the participation of men.

After a few more dates with Mike, Mary begins to feel confused about the situation. Lou and Murray cajole her into confiding in them with a pseudo-feminist argument about women wanting men to be more sensitive and sharing but then not telling them anything personal. After Mary tells them she's been out with Mike two or three times and had fun but that he's never become romantic with her, Murray exclaims, "Maybe Ted *is* right about him!" To which Mary replies with some disgust, "*This* is why women don't confide in men!" Later, in her apartment, Mary and Phyllis attempt to discuss how they feel about their own and each other's interest in Mike. After Phyllis leaves, Mike arrives, but Phyllis returns in time for Mike to tell Mary and Phyllis that he's back with his former fiancée, Sharon. As the shots cross-cut between Mike alone in the frame and Mary and Phyllis sharing a frame, Mike suggests they all get together sometime.

"Sure," Mary says dryly. "Sometime you and Sharon, and Phyllis and I can all go out dancing." With that, Mike exits, leaving Phyllis to console a not really upset Mary. "In your own peculiar way, Phyllis," Mary says, "you really care about me." Putting her head on Mary's shoulder, Phyllis replies, "Care about you, Mary? I 'wuv' you!" as the episode comes to a close. A coda finds Mary in the newsroom with Murray, asking him if he's "ever had a meaningful relationship with a woman that wasn't physical." "Yes," Murray says, "with my wife." In "Ménage-à-Phyllis" textual references to same-sex behavior and non-sexual relationships between men and women combine with the eroticized quasi-maternal interactions between two women to construct a narrative that passes through heterosexuality (Phyllis and Mary as rivals for the just-separated Mike) and bisexuality (Phyllis as being close to Mike and Mary simultaneously), to resolve itself as a lesbian domestic sitcom narrative with Mary and Phyllis reunited and declaring their affection for each other in Mary's kitchen.

In a similar way, *Laverne and Shirley* (1976–83) often developed its lesbian narratives and queer pleasures by "passing through" heterosexuality and other forms of relationships with men in order to re-establish the emotional and erotic status quo of two women living and working together. Much of the audience pleasure in this series is bound up in seeing how various threats to maintaining Laverne and Shirley as a couple are overcome. Set in the late 1950s and early 1960s in Milwaukee and then Burbank, the lesbian dynamics of this series often went beyond its narrative construction to include working-class lesbian cultural codes that positioned Laverne as the (unwitting) butch and Shirley as the (repressed) femme.[31]

Living in a basement apartment and working as bottle cappers for Shotz Brewery in Milwaukee, the pair often talked about men and their relationships with them in opposing terms: Laverne wanted lots of sex with lots of men, Shirley wanted to marry a professional and settle down in a middle-class suburb. But while Laverne's sexual aggressivity and voracity are frequently shown, Shirley's desire for a conventional marriage is consistently cast as a hopeless goal. This was for class-jumping reasons certainly, but I would also contend this was done in order to keep the narrative lesbian. Shirley often seems programmed to repeat the American Dream party line for women in her position at the time. Perhaps she has become fixated on this suburban dream, and will accept no substitute, because it allows her to stay with Laverne while providing her with an approved heterosexualizing cover: "I haven't found the right man/my 'prince' yet." Indeed,

Shirley's favorite song is "High Hopes," from the film *A Hole in the Head.*

An episode involving the Shotz company psychiatrist literally analyzes and exposes Shirley's heterosexual cover-up. Entering the doctor's office with false bravado, Shirley flings around a scarf she clutches in her hand, as if to emphasize her femme-ininity: "All right Doctore [*sic*], do your worst to me! Sit up there in your ivory tower and pass judgment on me! But remember, down here life goes on, and we little people protect each other. So you can push us around all you like." Nervously and comically hyperdramatic, Shirley is already revealing her role-playing, her hiding something the doctor could "pass judgment on," and her need to be protected because of this.

Immediately, the doctor turns Shirley's attention to the picture of a house she drew as part of her psychiatric testing, telling her it's a "lovely house":

SHIRLEY: Split level, colonial, flagstone driveway, doorbell that chimes "High Hopes."

DOCTOR: And the dog you drew, is it a collie?

SHIRLEY: Prince? Yes. It should be Princess, though. But I didn't find out she was a girl doggie until she had her puppies.

DOCTOR: You know a lot about this house.

SHIRLEY: Well yes. I've thought a lot about it, you know. It's my dream home.

DOCTOR: I noticed one thing though—there's nobody in it.

SHIRLEY: There's nobody in my house? (takes the drawing from the doctor and frantically examines it) There must be somebody here. (laughs nervously) So you're right. There's nobody in it! That doesn't mean anything, does it? Does it? . . . Of course it means something, doesn't it? Everything means something! (starts to pound on her forehead with her fist) Let me think. Why wouldn't there be people in my house? Why . . . wouldn't . . . there . . . be . . . people . . . in . . . my . . . house?

Although she first offers the weak explanation that there are no people in her house because they are all vacationing in Disneyland, she has to admit to the psychiatrist, "Gee, I just had a bad thought, you know. Maybe it's all just a pipe dream. Maybe I never will get married and have puppies. I don't know. Tell me, doctor, do you think I'm doomed to a life of despair?" Desperately grasping the doctor's "It all depends" as "no," Shirley falls to her knees, thanks him profusely ("You don't know how relieved those words have made me feel"), and borrows his pencil so she can draw herself and her husband coming home from Disneyland onto her original picture.

The psychoanalytic setting for all this encourages us to see what is revealed here as fraught with hidden meanings. Even Shirley admits this: "Of course it means something, doesn't it? Everything means something." But the narrative cuts off the doctor's analysis with the suggestion that Shirley may or may not be "doomed to a life of despair" because she has constructed a fantasy of suburban life without a husband or children in it. The ambiguity here is provocative in light of the show's lesbian narrative structure and cultural coding. Shirley may be doomed to a life of despair if she continues to hold on to a heterosexual fantasy she clearly doesn't believe in or want. On the other hand, she may not be doomed, because this fantasy allows her to reject all men as somehow not good enough, so she can continue to live with Laverne — after all, her suburban "Prince" is really a "Princess."

Related to Shirley's gender confusion about the dog (the only figure she does draw in her house) is her slip of the tongue that connects her potential roles as (straight) wife and mother to a dog having puppies. Thus connected with both her unacknowledged desire for a lesbian "dream" household (just her and Princess), and the prospect of being the (doglike) mother of a straight household, the figure of the dog as articulated through Shirley's psychiatric test represents the dilemma both of her character and of the series's narrative: she/it *should* want to be heterosexual, she/it *tries* to be heterosexual, but the force of lesbian desire (of the character, in the text) is strong. It is strong enough to set in motion all manner of heterosexual cover-ups that seek to contain, defuse, redefine, or render invisible what would come out as undeniable lesbian desire in characters and queer pleasures in audiences. To take one example, Shirley is given a regular boyfriend, Carmine Ragusa, during the Milwaukee episodes, but he is generally kept at arm's length by the fantasy of a virginal and middle-class wedding that Shirley's episode with the psychiatrist calls into question. Perhaps tired of the pretense, the show's producers and writers decided to make Carmine Shirley's friend when she and Laverne move to California.

Like Shirley's fantasies of straight domestic bliss, Laverne's constant one-night stands might also be seen as a form of heterosexual cover-up, as they ultimately pose little threat to her living arrangement with Shirley. In the show's 1950s-1960s context, there is no danger Laverne will go off to live with any of the men she sees for one or two dates. And although Laverne's sexual behavior can be read as hyperheterosexual, it is also linked to codes of masculinity and/or (stereo)typical codes of lesbian butchness. Frequently, Laverne's trysts begin with her making the first physical moves, often with an appalled Shirley looking on. While the men involved usually respond with pleased surprise to this sexual aggressivity, the number of Laverne's brief encounters during the run of the series comes to suggest that either the men don't come back for more or that Laverne doesn't want them to come back. Either way, Laverne is also narratively let off the ultimate straight hook of marriage and family because audiences are encouraged to enjoy how her masculinized sexual behavior scares men off, or how it is farcically rendered as "trampy" or "bad girl" behavior.

Early in the series, Laverne's background as a high-school tough girl or "greaser" is often introduced in the form of members of her old girl gang, particularly Rosie Greenbaum. Episodes featuring Rosie explore the tensions that have developed between her and Laverne as a result of Rosie's pretentious behavior after she marries an upper-middle-class professional. Laverne sees Rosie's attitude as a betrayal of who she and Rosie were (and are), and the pair swiftly move from verbal insults to wrestling matches to express their frustrations. Most obviously, Rosie's betrayal is a class betrayal, but her girl-gang past with Laverne suggests her betrayal also concerns gender and sexuality: that is, heterosexual coupling in marriage versus women-bonding in pairs and groups.

Ultimately the series itself would place Shirley in Rosie's position, while providing Laverne with a steady boyfriend. But even these heterosexualizing narrative ploys were undercut by the accumulated force of the show's lesbian dynamics. As mentioned earlier, this lesbian atmosphere is established in *Laverne and Shirley* not only by how the program constructs the audience's emotional and erotic investment in its women-bonding narrative(s), but also by its frequent use of various cultural codes of lesbianism, which might be read as conventionally heterocentrist stereotyping, as lesbian culture-specific, or as some combination of both. The group of episodes that have Laverne and Shirley in the Army, for example, play on codes of the butch sergeant and her troop of Amazons in a manner that allows straight- and queer-identified viewers, in their different ways, to enjoy the proceedings as lesbian comedy. These episodes also offer the

spectacle of both Laverne and Shirley being transformed into masculinized women/butches during basic training, and then into hyperfem-
inized women/femmes when they are cast as prostitutes in an Army
hygiene film.

But most often, Laverne is the masculine/butch of the pair, while
Shirley is the feminine/femme. The lesbianism linked to these positions comes very close to the series' narrative surface a few times during its seven-year run. In one episode, after the pair win a plane trip
for two in a Schotz Brewery lottery, Laverne admits she's afraid of flying. Shirley convinces her to face her fears, but Laverne panics once
the plane takes off, accidentally knocking out the male copilot and
pilot. Taking over for the pilot, Laverne puts on his cap while she follows the radio instructions of an air controller. As she clutches her
trademark scarf, Shirley returns to the passenger cabin, pretending to
be a volunteer stewardess ("Perhaps you've heard of us? Candy-strip-
ers of the air.") in order to find a passenger who knows how to fly.
When the real stewardess enters and tells everyone to prepare for a
"crash landing," Shirley rushes to the cockpit, falls to her knees, says
"Good-bye, Laverne," and gives her partner a passionate kiss. "We'll
talk about that later, Shirl," replies a startled Laverne. But Shirley
persists in expressing her deep feelings for Laverne as she squeezes
into the pilot's seat so they can "die together." Touched by Shirley's
sentiments, Laverne asks her if she remembers what she wrote in Laverne's high-school yearbook. As the plane descends, the pair recite
in unison:

> If in heaven we don't meet,
> Hand-in-hand we'll bear the heat.
> And if it ever gets too hot,
> Pepsi-Cola hits the spot!

On the last line, the plane touches down while Laverne and Shirley
scream and hold on to each other. As it turns out, the pilot has revived
just in time to help with the landing, so the women's accomplishments
are somewhat tarnished by male intervention, although the pilot calls
what Laverne did "heroic." Of course, Laverne never does talk to
Shirley about that kiss.

But she *does* "marry" her: twice, in fact. The first time is the result
of another contest win. Shirley has entered a contest whose first prize
is a wedding dress and a weekend at the Hotel Pfister. What she
doesn't think through is how she'll be able to fulfill the contest re-
quirement that the winner actually be married in the dress before en-

joying her honeymoon at the Pfister. Enter Laverne, who is initially enthusiastic about spending the weekend with Shirley, and who only needs a little persuading to be talked into becoming her groom. What follows is a series of farcical situations that find Laverne and Shirley, in their wedding tuxedo and gown, trying to convince everyone they are indeed husband and wife.

More remarkable is Laverne's second "marriage" to Shirley, because it takes place during, and actually in the place of, Shirley's marriage to Army surgeon Walter Meany. Coming near the end of Cindy Williams's participation in the show, this wedding also becomes the climax of Laverne and Shirley's long and loving relationship. Up to this point, the program found a number of narrative excuses not to show Walter Meany to the audience, that is, not to make incarnate a major threat to the show's lesbian narrative/queer pleasures. And we never do get to see Walter, because on the eve of the wedding he is involved in an accident that puts him in a head and body cast. Held in the intensive care ward of an Army hospital and presided over by a uniformed Army chaplain (which reminds viewers of Laverne and Shirley's stint as WACs), the wedding proceeds on schedule, with Laverne as both maid of honor and groom. Coming to the part of the service where rings are exchanged, Laverne stands behind the propped-up Walter, slips her hand through the crook of his arm, and places the ring on Shirley's finger. Still clasping hands as the chaplain says "I now pronounce you man and wife," Laverne and Shirley look tenderly at each other for a moment across Walter's immobilized body before realizing the implications and unclasping their hands. After kissing Walter, however, Shirley immediately turns to hug and kiss Laverne, as Walter is excluded from the shot.[32]

In spite of this marriage, Laverne and Shirley (and the program) were kept together a while longer by narrative ploys that had Walter constantly on special assignment.[33] When Cindy Williams became pregnant, the show looked as if it would follow *I Love Lucy*'s pattern and use a cast member's maternity to revitalize the bonds between women characters. As with Lucy and Ethel, Shirley first announces her pregnancy to Laverne. After this, the two of them go through various prenatal experiences together as a couple, something Laverne does again later when a somewhat feminized Sarge shows up pregnant and without a husband. But when Williams left to have her baby, she decided not to return to the show. With Williams/Shirley gone, the program became *Laverne and Company*. In a manner reminiscent of the last seasons of *The Mary Tyler Moore Show* and *Kate and Allie*,

Laverne and Company's narratives and characters are heterosexualized: Laverne is given a muscular stuntman for a boyfriend; the Monroesque starlet next door gets to drop by more often with news of her latest conquest; Carmine becomes engaged.[34]

Actually Shirley's absence from the show left it with little hope of reviving the fundamental source of its audience appeal, since Shirley was always the character who most successfully negotiated the threatening lesbian narrative spaces between being a heterosexual character functioning within the structures of lesbian narrative, being a subtextual lesbian within the codes of straight and lesbian (sub)cultural connotation, and being denotatively marked as a "real" lesbian character by the text. In the Army hygiene film episode, it is, significantly, Shirley's acting partner who makes a point of telling her he's gay after she warns him that she doesn't want any onscreen romance to continue offscreen. This being the case, it becomes clear that Shirley and her costar can only pantomime straight lust under their heterosexually pornographic stage names, "Shirley Love" and "Johnny Pulse." This sense of straight role-playing with its attempted repression of the queer is most intensely centered around Shirley, but this role-playing is also crucial to maintaining the queer pleasures of *Laverne and Shirley* for many viewers, as it camouflages what is lesbian about the program.

I will conclude this chapter with *Designing Women* (1986–present), not only because it is one of the most recent long-running lesbian sitcoms, but because its 1991–92 season clearly revealed an important point about these shows: the chemistry between the women characters/actors is ultimately more important to maintaining the lesbian dynamics in these shows than is the presence or absence of (straight) men. Going beyond the idea of men as potential threats to its community of women, *Designing Women* has been rather offhand about introducing, and then marginalizing or eliminating, the men who date or marry its women characters. Overall, this indifferent treatment of men and "compulsory heterosexuality" makes it clear that the narrative fact of straight romance and marriage does not necessarily heterosexualize lesbian sitcoms any more than being married makes actual lesbians straight.[35]

Until its 1991–92 season, *Designing Women* was popular with both critics and the public for having one of the most dynamic ensemble casts on American television: Dixie Carter (Julia Sugarbaker), Delta Burke (Suzanne Sugarbaker), Annie Potts (Mary Jo Shively), and Jean Smart (Charlene Stillfield). Even regular Meshach Taylor's Anthony

Bouvier, the Sugarbaker interior design firm's delivery person and general assistant, was considered "one of the girls" (as Mary Jo puts it) and Suzanne's "girlfriend." Alice Ghostley, joining the cast later in the series run as the Sugarbakers' outrageous Aunt Bernice, rounded out the original ensemble of women and one (subtextual?) gay man.

With this cast, *Designing Women* ran through the entire spectrum of characteristic lesbian sitcom situations. Charlene's pregnancy and the birth of daughter Olivia largely took place in the absence of Charlene's Air Force officer husband, Bill, who was away on overseas duty. With the support of her coworkers/friends, Charlene has the child, returns to work, and finds a nanny to take care of Olivia on the floor above the firm's main office. With day nursery, offices, and stockrooms located in Julia's home, the series goes most other lesbian sitcoms one better by combining work and domestic spaces, and marking both as female, thereby intensifying the primacy of these women's relationships with each other. Indeed, *Designing Women* offers a matriarchal vision combining the spheres of work and home that patriarchal capitalism insists on keeping separate, gendered, and differently valued (male/work/important, female/home/trivial).

This matriarchal network of work and maternity expanded beyond biological mothers Charlene, Mary Jo, and Julia to include Suzanne, in an episode in which she accidentally puts some of Charlene's breast milk (stored in the office refrigerator for Olivia's feedings) into her coffee. Denying she used the milk, Suzanne yells, "What do you think I am — a pervert?" What "pervert" might mean here is taken up in a later sequence at a restauraunt when Suzanne, photographed in two shots with Charlene, says she thinks their waiter Ian is "a homosexual." When Mary Jo returns from the bathroom, she overhears Ian's name and asks who he is. "Our homosexual waiter," Charlene answers, taking her cue from Suzanne. This suggestive pairing of Charlene and Suzanne occurs a number of times in the series, as does the coupling of Julia and Mary Jo. Among other things, Mary Jo and Julia have danced together while dressed as a (male) chef and a restaurant hostess, and while costumed as Bette Davis and Joan Crawford in *Whatever Happened To Baby Jane?* (the latter in the "The Strange Case of Clarence and Anita" episode).

Since Suzanne constantly comments about "homosexuals" during the series' run, it makes sense that she would be the character who is most immediately involved with the "real" lesbian character in *Designing Women*'s "lesbian episode." Mistaking the "coming out" of Eugenia Weeks, a friend from her beauty pageant days, as part of the

Southern tradition of being presented as a straight, marriageable woman at a debutante ball, Suzanne agrees to go to a banquet with Eugenia. When the other women at the firm clarify matters, Suzanne is appalled, and asks them to come with her to a bar-restaurant where she is supposed to meet Eugenia. Certain it is a lesbian bar, the women attempt to play it cool, but end up acting awkward, particularly Mary Jo, who at one point asks Julia to hold her hand and pretend to be her girlfriend. Finally confronting each other in a health club sauna (where another woman understands their remarks as part of a lesbian love spat), Suzanne reconciles with Eugenia because she sees they have so much in common.

But while Suzanne was reconciling with Eugenia, Delta Burke found herself more and more at odds with her producers, writers, and costars. After a series of charges alleging that Burke's diva-like temperament and demands were disruptive to the atmosphere on the set, Burke countercharged that she was being badly treated (primarily because of weight gains) and was underappreciated. Many members of *Designing Women*'s cast, crew, and production staff felt Burke's new attitude was attributable to the influence of her husband, Gerald Rainey (star of the sitcom *Major Dad*, in which he plays a Marine officer).[36] The situation came to a head during the 1990–91 season. While the series achieved its highest Nielsen ratings ever (it was the ninth-ranked show), and Burke was nominated for an Emmy award for "best actress in a comedy series" (something no other cast member had achieved), *Designing Women* executives decided to fire Burke. Soon afterward Jean Smart announced that she would leave the show to pursue other acting projects and spend more time with her family.

Clearly hoping to retain the same type of family bonding between the women characters, the show's producers cast Julia Duffy as Suzanne's and Julia's cousin Allison Sugarbaker, and Jan Hooks as Charlene's cousin Carlene. The hour-long 1991–92 season premiere to introduce the new characters left critics and audiences disappointed: Allison seemed shrill and aloof, and Carlene a colorless copy of Charlene. Then, in what seemed an attempt to more quickly integrate the new characters into the existing ensemble, an episode was aired early in the season that made the "hidden" source of the series's narrative pleasures more overt through a "women marrying women" leitmotiv running throughout the episode.

Carlene's gratitude to Mary Jo for helping her during her first weeks in Atlanta and at the firm touches off this theme. Rushing downstairs and into the combination living room-main office, Carlene excitedly says, "Mary Jo, you are just the best girlfriend I ever had. I mean it! If you were a man, I'd marry you." Then, as if seriously considering the issue, she looks offscreen, and her next line — "But, you know, Julia, I'd find you very attractive, too." — concludes over a shot of Julia smiling. Standing between Julia and Mary Jo, who are seated on a sofa, Carlene continues: "It would be a tough decision. Mary Jo or Julia? I can't decide! What do you think, Allison?" And while Allison sarcastically remarks, "I think you need a date — bad!" she petulantly snaps, "Am not!" when Mary Jo advises Carlene not to pay attention to Allison because "she's just mad because none of us want to marry her." With no transition, Carlene replies, "Well, gosh, you know my divorce is just barely final. I don't think I'd be comfortable dating another man at this point." Given its context, Carlene's non sequitur implies she would, and does, feel comfortable dating (or marrying) another woman.

But since this cannot be expressed directly in the surface narrative except as a joke, Carlene finds herself constructing an elaborate scheme with Mary Jo in which they enlist Anthony as Carlene's date in order to thwart Carlene's ex-husband, who wants to remarry her. Although he skeptically views their plan as being "like something Lucy and Ethel would do,"[37] Anthony lowers his voice and plays his part, even in the face of a surprise encounter with Allison at the restaurant where he, Carlene, and her ex-husband are meeting:

ANTHONY: Carlene and I have been dating for some time.

ALLISON: I don't believe it.

ANTHONY: It was a secret.

ALLISON: I cannot believe that this woman blows into town five minutes ago and already she's got a best friend and a boyfriend. Not the ones I would choose, but still . . . I mean, I think I'm attractive, but I don't have a best friend. I don't have a boyfriend. And for some reason, none of the women at work want to marry me!

That the prospect of marrying a woman — or having a woman want to marry her — is finally more important to Allison than having a best friend or a boyfriend becomes clear in the last sequence of the episode. While the narrative works to have Carlene (re)place her semiserious talk of marrying a woman within the terms of homosociality by having her tell Mary Jo, "You just got a little carried away with that female camaraderie. So what?," Allison remains in a less assimilable position. The frustration she expresses after discovering that Anthony is not Carlene's boyfriend goes beyond this specific case of being lied to by the other three women (and Anthony) to obliquely address certain bigger lies about the slippery straightness of characters and narratives on *Designing Women*: "Wait! Wait a minute! Are you telling me that you two are not going out? Oh, right. So first you weren't, then you were, and now you aren't. That's great. You know, you people are just messing with me. And I would like to tell you something: I wouldn't marry any of you girls if you begged me!"

As it turns out, both Allison and the audience are finally being "messed with" by the "first you weren't, then you were, now you aren't" presentation of the women (and Anthony, for that matter) on the show. Because while this episode's narrative tries to contain its lesbian dynamics by initially contextualizing the discussion of marriage in straight terms (Carlene's "If I was a man . . ."); Allison's obsessive returning to Mary Jo's remark (about how none of the other women at the firm want to marry her) takes the idea of women marrying women beyond its original jokey straight context and into a textual (rather than subtextual) queer space that links narrative, character, and audience pleasures. But perhaps Allison's moment of lesbian anger and frustration in the face of coy homosociality proved too much for the character and the newly recast series to bear. At the end of the 1991–92 season, executive producer Linda Bloodworth-Thomason announced that Julia Duffy/Allison would not be returning for another season. While telling the press that Duffy "did a spectacular job in a very difficult role," the character was being dropped from the series because "the network didn't feel the chemistry was right."[38]

I would contend that the chemistry wasn't right not only because Duffy/Allison wasn't able to establish a sisterly rapport with the rest of the cast but also because Allison was in danger of forcing *Designing Women* to "come out."[39] Duffy's Allison never really had a chance of connecting with women characters whose bonds are finally, if not permanently, heterosexualized by the end of each episode's narrative. But if the lesbian sentiments of characters such as Allison and the narratives built around them were to become more denotative and less connotative on series such as *Designing Women*, or if they were not explained as cases of women living, working, or otherwise banding together for basically economic or blood-relations reasons (as is the case with *Kate and Allie, Alice, The Golden Girls, Designing Women, Babes, Phyllis, It's a Living, Roseanne, Sugar 'n' Spice,* and *Laverne and Shirley*)—that is, if these sitcom narratives depicted women forming emotional, intellectual, and erotic relationships with each other out of choice rather than from necessity—what is threatening about these women-centered programs would be in danger of overwhelming the queer pleasures many audiences unwittingly experience as they watch women characters together.

CHAPTER FOUR

The Gay Straight Man

Jack Benny and The Jack Benny Program

Grandmother to grandson after a tense family dinner which includes his male partner: "Maybe he can fix my radio. It hasn't worked since Jack Benny went off the air."

From An Early Frost, *a television film about coming out and AIDS[1]*

For forty years, Jack Benny was America's favorite feminine straight man—in both senses of the word "straight." However, since patriarchal cultures can't comfortably support for very long the paradox of a straight male with mannerisms traditionally coded as feminine, it is perhaps more accurate to say that for forty years Jack Benny was actually America's favorite fag.[2] As Benny's comic star image took shape through work in vaudeville, radio, film, and television, it gradually became associated with qualities conventionally considered unmasculine: vanity (about his blue eyes, his hair, his age); coyness; excessive hand and arm gestures; a loose, bouncy walk; a high-pitched nervous giggle; an interest in playing the violin; a lack of aggressive sexual desire for women; and a general lack of aggressiveness in his dealings with other people, except in the form of frequent so-called catty remarks. Walter Kerr, reviewing Benny's stage show in 1963, commented that Benny's comic persona "somehow manages to become both patience AND the monument all primped into one," adding:

> He simply enters like a floorwalker who has been promoted to the best floor, and he has come, basically, to keep an eye on you. He clasps his hands together as though to say, "What can I do for you?" or perhaps "Who stole my muff?" He is languid and lethal and rueful and baleful and at all times ready to bite his lip in embarrassment, should anything untoward turn up.[3]

63

Given this character profile, it seems remarkable that after years at the margins of mainstream mass culture as a prissy, tragic, or evil figure, the feminine gay character could be made a star by Benny and his collaborators.

On closer inspection, however, the terms of this stardom usually required Benny's character to repeatedly play out comic situations constructed to displace him as the center of power. Constantly beset by a fast-talking cast of characters intent upon sadistically humiliating him, Benny's comic persona—whom I'll call "Jack" from here on—was placed in the position of masochistically feeding the "gang" straight lines, or uttering self-deprecating remarks, or resorting to desperate, ineffectual retorts, like "Now cut that out!" and "Don't be so fresh!" As Benny staff writer and biographer Milt Josefsberg explains the situation: "Jack was, in truth, the stooge for all the supporting players. . . . And it was they, not he, who got the laughs."[4] In his autobiography (contained within a biography by daughter, Joan Benny) Benny discusses various "masochistic stunts" he and his writers would construct for Jack, including a publicity scheme that helped encourage the already strong conflation of Benny and Jack. This was the "I Can't Stand Jack Benny Because . . . " (originally the "Why I Hate Jack Benny") contest conducted in the 1940s, of which Benny says, "I knew if we went through with this idea it would be the most extreme limit to which I had ever carried the masochism bit. Did I really want to publicly humiliate myself just for laughs?"[5] The answer to this question was yes, as the contest went on as scheduled.

Strategies such as these constructed Benny's "sissy" or "effeminate" character to work comfortably and conventionally within long-established Western cultural traditions that try to neutralize and contain the threat of the unmasculine or feminine man by making him the butt of homophobic laughter. As Benny once remarked, "The minute I come on, even the most hen-pecked guy in the audience feels good."[6] Of the three major Benny biographies, and the combination biography-autobiography, only Josefsberg's *The Jack Benny Show* directly addresses the topic of Benny and gayness, in a chapter titled "Benny's Walk" that ends with a rather startling anecdote about events during rehearsal breaks of a show Benny did with Marilyn Monroe. According to Josefsberg, director Ralph Levy made Monroe repeat her famous walk a number of times for the enjoyment of the crew, under the pretext it was necessary rehearsal. Hearing the crew's off-color joking about Monroe, Benny said, "I don't know why everyone raves about Marilyn. I've got a pretty attractive ass myself." In the middle of the giggles that ensued, according to Josefsberg, the "company fag lisped, 'You can thay that again!' " — and Benny and the crew went into hysterics.[7] Though Josefsberg is careful to note that everyone realized the comment was meant to be taken as a joke, it is clear the real joke is on the "company fag," and through him, on the gay elements in Benny's comic persona.

While the biographies by Benny's manager, Irving Fein, his wife, Mary Livingstone, and the autobiography by Benny and his daughter, Joan Benny, contain nothing as revelatory as Josefsberg's chapter, they include material suggesting that even for those closest to Benny, the gay elements of Benny's star image became one important (sub)-text for their narrations of his life. Fein's biography, for example, offers the observation that when Benny was a child, "the other kids made fun of him because he threw the ball like a girl. Later, when Jack became a star," Fein continues, "everybody teased him about walking like a girl, too."[8] The Livingstone biography, written in collaboration with her brother Hilliard Marks and Marcia Borie, makes much of Benny's going off with the women at parties when guests would divide themselves into same-sex conversation groups: "I've had enough of this," Benny is quoted as saying to the men at one gathering, "I'm going over to talk to the pretty people."[9] "Most men would have thought it *unmacho* to be so sweet," Johnny Carson adds later about Benny's fondness for socializing with women.[10]

Both the Fein and the Livingstone biographies reveal that Benny's favorite phrase to direct at men he felt an affection for was "Kiss my ass!," and both books are notable for describing Benny's vaudeville days as being filled with "handsome" or "good-looking" young men who were his partners or admirers. Many of these men are quoted as returning the compliment by praising Benny's physical beauty and charm. Along these lines, perhaps the most remarkable revelation about how the gayness of Benny's star image translated itself into biographical erotics comes with the treatment of Benny's long friendship with George Burns. Pivoting around Benny's occasional drag performances with George as the latter's partner and wife, Gracie Allen, the biographies, taken together, sketch out a compelling sadomasochistic scenario in which Burns is constantly inflicting upon Benny various forms of verbal and physical (supposedly humorous) public humiliation. In response to all this, Benny consistently rewards Burns with fits of prolonged, intense, and even incapacitating laughter that can only be labeled "orgasmic" as they are described in the three biographies. Dutifully recorded in these books is Benny's one major attempt to outdo Burns with a practical joke involving Benny standing nude on a hotel room bed with a book on his head, a glass of water in one hand, and a rose in the other.

As it turns out, Burns can also be added to the list of men who were taken by Benny's looks and his charm:

> When I first met Jack, he was such a beautiful man. . . . He was so handsome . . . so slim . . . so suave. . . . He had those blue eyes and that velvet voice. . . . Well, he was a knockout on stage. . . . He looked fragile with those thin wrists . . . the way he touched his face . . . his baby-smooth skin. He seemed so vulnerable, you wanted to take him home and adopt him.[11]

That these tender, erotic sentiments are recorded in Mary Livingstone's biography makes them even more provocative, particularly when coupled with an anecdote about Benny that Burns told on *The Arsenio Hall Show* (January 2–3, 1990). Recalling one of Benny's drag performances as Gracie in London, Burns remembered how carefully Benny shaved his legs and fussed with his dress. After the performance, according to Burns, Livingstone called the hotel and asked Burns to tell Benny to "take off the dress—the show's over." "Benny really enjoyed wearing it," Burns quickly added.[12]

Benny's conventionally "feminine" mannerisms and his supposed penchant for drag become the basis for a number of anecdotes in the biographies. And, as with Burns's *Arsenio Hall* tall tale, the line between Benny's stage character and his private life is often playfully blurred in these stories. Perhaps the most repeated and most representative of these anecdotes is the story of bandleader Phil Harris watching Benny walk away from him, then turning to a band member and commenting "You know what, Frankie? You could put a dress on that guy and take him anywhere!"[13] An intriguing variant on this situation was performed on one of Benny's radio broadcasts (November 18, 1945) when boxer Joe Louis asks Mary Livingstone the ever-popular question, "Who was that lady I saw you with?" "That was no lady," Mary replies. "That was Jack—he always walks that way!"[14] It is no accident, then, that Josefsberg titled his chapter on Benny and gayness "Jack's Walk," because Benny most insistently and consistently encouraged a gay reading of his comic persona by exploiting this walk and building it into a character trademark through jokes about it on his radio shows, carefully planned entrances and exits on his television and stage shows, and gags constructed around it for his guest appearances on other programs. One such guest appearance on

The Lucy Show has Lucille Ball glide out of an office after asking Jack to "walk this way." Jack watches her exit, pauses, and remarks "I always do." Josefsberg's "Jack's Walk" chapter is intriguing for the complex network of queer associations it pulls together around this spectacularized walk: everything from Jack as Gracie, to Benny's *Charley's Aunt* costar Laird Cregar's admitting he was gay, to the "company fag" anecdote mentioned earlier.[15]

After Benny's walk and his feminine/effeminate body language in general, only the quality of cheapness is more strongly associated with Benny's star image. Taken together, these two defining character traits suggest a pathology of sexual dysfunction in which unacceptable gay behavior/desire has been displaced and avaricious activity substituted for it—avarice being an excessive or aberrant behavior better tolerated and understood by capitalist, patriarchal culture. In this context, the comic hysteria Jack displays when, for example, Rochester takes—or threatens to take—money from Jack's pants pockets or from his mattress, accumulates intriguing psychosexual and social dimensions, bound up as it is with codes of gayness, Jewishness, and blackness.[16] It is worth noting here that Jewish actor Benny Rubin was originally set for the part eventually played by Eddie Anderson, which metamorphosed from train porter to valet to housekeeper-companion.[17] Perhaps the suggestive juncture of miserliness and gayness explains why one of Benny's few successful film roles was in *Charley's Aunt* (1941, Warners, Archie Mayo), impersonating a rich middle-aged woman in order to help two straight men with their romantic affairs.

By the time of *Charley's Aunt*, years of capitalizing on the potential for self- and other-inflicted put-down humor within the matrix of effeminacy and miserliness had firmly established Benny's star image as implicitly, if uneasily, gay. Benny's radio program, which began in 1932, became the vehicle for establishing this star image as it constructed a broad queer context for the star's comic persona. However, since radio listeners could not see Benny performing, and so were deprived of the sight of his walk and gesturing, these radio programs relied upon aural codes (descriptive language, vocal pitch, violin music, human noises, double-entendre dialogue, meaningful pauses, etc.) to convey the gayness of Benny's character, which had been developing gradually from the actor's 1920s–1930s stage and screen image as a tuxedoed "suave comedian, dry humorist and . . . master of ceremonies."[18]

Beginning with a 1950 special, the television version of *The Jack Benny Program* (1950–65, CBS/NBC) continued to present Benny as a feminine gay/effeminate star through his Jack character. Indeed, many of the television episodes were little more than reworkings of the radio programs—the major difference being that through television a mass audience could now see the spectacle of Jack's walk and mannerisms, rather than just imagine them. Therefore, with the understanding that the series' basic format, character types, and ideological agenda regarding gayness remained consistent from radio to television, I will focus my attention on the Benny radio program, with an occasional mention of the television series.

In one telling casting move, Mary Livingstone did not play Jack's wife on either the radio or the television show. Instead, her character developed into a vaguely defined wisecracking cast member whose primary function is to needle Jack about his looks, his vanity, his cheapness, and, on those rare occasions they went out, about what a hopeless date he was. The sound of Mary laughing at Jack is perhaps the key signifier defining her relationship with him on the show. Speaking of Jack and the Mary Livingstone character in his autobiography, Benny says:

> Did you know that the fictional Jack Benny, my character on radio and television, was a bachelor? . . . The fictional Mary Livingstone never was my girlfriend. She was a kind of heckler-secretary. She always had a sarcastic edge that colored our relationship.[19]

Later in the radio program's 23-year run, as well as during the television series' 15-year run, Mary was abetted in her verbal emasculation of Jack by other women, such as a pair of switchboard operators who were often even more graphic in their comments about Jack's various physical and character shortcomings: he'd usually have them pay their own way on dates, after which he'd offer them lukewarm kisses. Frequently described by Jack himself were dates with various butch "he-women" such as Myrtle Minklehoffer, who was a deep-sea diver and wrestler and who had "shoulders like Victor Mature." "Oh, I made *believe* I was a Don Juan," Benny said of his character, "but I had stupid affairs with telephone operators and waitresses and even these never amounted to much."[20]

Constructed around more pointed gay innuendo were Jack's relationships with the male members of what was called his radio and television "gang"—particularly with the namesake characters played by bandleader Phil Harris, "boy" sopranos Kenny Baker and Dennis

Day, and manservant/chauffeur Eddie ("Rochester") Anderson. Indeed, by the mid-1940s, many of Benny's radio programs begin to sound like early versions of *The Boys in the Band*, with Mary Livingstone as the token witty "fag hag," "fag moll," or, as Imamu Amiri Baraka labels her in his play *Jello*, a "TV/radio-dikey."[21] Interestingly, the radio shows are at their most suggestive about gayness when performed at military bases, as they often were during World War II. During a 1944 tour of the South Pacific to entertain U.S. troops, Benny did a routine about his experiences as a sailor in World War I:

> In those days, they used to place you according to what you did in civilian life. If you were a mailman, you were put in the infantry; if you were a cowboy, you went into the cavalry, and if you were a mechanic, you became an engineer. How I ever ended up on a *fairy* [sic] boat, I'll never know![22]

Without the implicit, widespread public understanding of Benny's comic persona as homosexual, there is no joke here. This brazen double-entendre gay-connotative joking was perhaps more permissible given a certain "men together under pressure" wartime ethos. As Allan Bérubé documents in the "GI Drag: A Gay Refuge" chapter of *Coming Out Under Fire: The History of Gay Men and Women in World War II*, elements of gay culture found their way into almost all areas of military entertainments during the war. Although gay material, most notably female impersonation, could create tensions within the ranks, a strong current of heterosexualizing rhetoric from military spokespersons and the press attempted to keep any queerness in the realm of unspoken connotation.[23] In this context, the suggestive gayness of Benny's comic persona could be pushed to its limits.

From the beginning, however, conventional comic effeminate or gay elements were apparent on Benny radio broadcasts. The show broadcast on February 11, 1934, for example, featured Jack providing gossipy tabloid news flashes about such events as how large-footed star Greta Garbo's arrival in New York increased wholesale orders for shoes in the city. Jack also attempts to fabricate a feud between Garbo and Katharine Hepburn by reporting that while in New York Garbo is taking in some plays and would like to see Hepburn in *The Lake*. Hepburn, Jack reports, says she "would like to see Garbo in the Hudson River." "Could this be jealousy?" he coyly asks his radio audience. Immediately after Jack's news flashes, Mary tells him she has a news flash of her own: she is going on vacation. "Jealous?" Mary asks Jack, thereby placing him in the position of one of the two supposedly feuding actresses. During the ensuing discussion of vacations, one orchestra member reveals that Jack's hat has been hanging in a speakeasy for thirteen years. "Oh, you nasty man, you!" Jack peevishly retorts.

At the start of a 1937 broadcast (February 8) announcer Don Wilson informs listeners that Jack has just finished collecting the autographs of three "suave lover-types"—Clark Gable, John Barrymore, and Robert Taylor. After this introduction, Jack comes on to add comments about Phil Harris's good looks, while also referring to Kenny Baker as "a little dumb, but cute." A bizarre case of gender-blurring on a 1938 show (March 27) involved "cute" Kenny Baker being confused with Kate Smith as Jack has a slip of the tongue, announcing after a musical number, "That was 'This Time It's Real,' sung by Kenny—uh—Kate Smith." After this slip, Baker is quickly on the phone to Jack, worried that Smith will replace him and jealously demanding the same ermine wrap Smith has requested of Jack. "I never knew why," biographer Josefsberg comments, "but Jack always insisted that his singer[s] be . . . tenor[s] . . . [with] high-pitched voices."[24]

As suggested earlier, by the time of Benny's appearance in the film *Charley's Aunt*, the show's gay subtext often became the text. It was around this time that rumors about Benny's own sexuality became more persistent, according to Josefsberg.[25] During one interview, Benny recalled how a certain critic, writing about his performance in the film, "claimed that so much of my own personality came through that I should have been billed as Jacqueline Benny."[26] Benny's radio programs of the period did their part in reinforcing this feminine gay image, while also linking other male characters in the cast with such conventional codes of gayness as cross-gender identification and behavior. On the November 5, 1941, program Don Wilson introduces Jack as a "versatile movie star" who has run the gamut from "leading man in *Love Thy Neighbor* to leading lady in *Charley's Aunt*." While Jack takes some pains to correct Don by asserting he is "really a man masquerading as a woman" in the film, their discussion quickly turns to wearing women's clothes, as Don admits his own corset is as "tight and hot" as the one Jack wore in *Charley's Aunt*. Jack, for his part, insists he looks "cute as the dickens" and even "adorable" in his *Charley's Aunt* drag—attractive enough, in fact, to get a date with costar Jack Oakie, even though the date ended badly when Jack was forced to walk home after Oakie got fresh. "And he can keep his mink coat!" Jack adds angrily at the memory. Mary, however, is quick to reveal that Oakie is still interested in taking Jack to Honolulu.

Allusions to drag activity and displays of (ef)feminized male vanity continued as mainstays of the Benny radio program throughout the 1940s and 1950s, with Phil Harris and Dennis Day often implicated in the show's gay text through these expedients. On a 1942 broadcast (April 14), Jack compliments Phil on his tan, in response to which Phil lisps out, "Tomorrow I'm going to do my back," before proceeding to make disparaging remarks about Jack's physique. "Say, when I played Hamlet in *To Be or Not To Be*," Jack remarks defensively, "I wore tights and had great legs. Didn't I, Mary?" After Mary fails to feed his vanity, Jack remarks, "You're just jealous like all those Hollywood women because I've got such great gams!"

Another 1942 show (March 15) had Jack worried the entire cast would quit when the Baxter Beauty Clay people offer them a better radio contract. After bitterly contemplating the irony of the "gang's" being lured away by a company that makes a product he uses himself, Jack confronts each cast member. He is thwarted in his attempt to shame Dennis into staying by reminding him of the raise he was recently given when Mary remarks, "Some raise, you put high heels on his shoes!" To which Dennis adds, "I've turned my ankles ten times this week!" Phil decides he wouldn't leave Jack for "all the beauty clay in the world." "Though heaven knows I need it!" he adds. Along the same lines, an earlier broadcast opens with Phil's mother scolding him for spending so much time "primping" his hair. "Oh, it's a mess!" Phil remarks, in fey distress. "Can I borrow your curling iron?" "What happened to yours?" Mom asks. Phil is finally forced to admit he ruined his during a "weenie bake" at the beach.

Frequently cast as "female" in similar situations over the radio years, Harris's character quickly became Jack's most overtly gay compatriot and rival, with Phil's alcoholism offering a parallel to Jack's miserliness in respect to their characters' sexual pathology.[27] Harris's wife, the actress Alice Faye, is often mentioned on the show as being married to Phil, just as Mary occasionally has dates with Jack and was also known to be his wife offstage. Ultimately, however, Faye functions for Harris's comic character much as Mary (and other women) did for Jack's: as a convenient heterosexualizing cover that allows performers and listeners alike to negotiate a relatively untroubled and untroubling comic space from which to exploit and disempower gayness as "just a joke."

Once or twice the radio programs come intriguingly close to exposing the text's work in constructing heterosexist narrative cover-ups involving Mary, Alice, Jack, and Phil. One such moment occurs when Jack and Mary reenact the beginning of their courtship, when Jack met Mary while she clerked at a department store.

MARY: I sell ladies' hosiery and things.

JACK: Just what I need, ladies' hosiery and things. (then, after a
             pause) For my sister.

On another program, Jack decides he will direct, produce, write, and act in a film of his life. Laughing, Mary adds, "I'll lend you my girdle; then you can be your own leading lady." After considering this for a moment, Jack decides "No, that would be going too far." Phil has a similar moment on an earlier show when he meets Jack at a drugstore coffee shop. Jack immediately notices that Phil's slacks look strange, as they button up the side. "Well, I'll be darned," Phil remarks calmly. "I put on a pair of Alice's."

But even outside such outrageous textual "moments of truth," the program builds up a dense, sexually suggestive atmosphere around Jack and Phil's relationship. The gay elements in their radio relationship were often reinforced by their appearances in stage versions of the show performed during the 1940s. One stage routine has Jack puzzling over how a woman like Alice Faye could have married Phil. "Well, wait a minute, what's wrong with that?" demands Phil. "I've got a right to be married, ain't I?" "That's not what I mean, Phil," Jack replies. "What I can't understand is the proposal. How did the proposal take place?" "Oh, the romance. . . . You want a little romance, huh?" Phil asks. When Jack replies "yes," Phil launches into a description of being surrounded by "beautiful blue eyes," "gorgeous wavy blonde hair," and "luscious lips." "What would you do in a case like that?" Phil demands of Jack. "I don't know, Phil," Jack replies. "I guess I'd get down on one knee and propose." "That's exactly what Alice did!" Phil exclaims, thereby placing Jack in the same position vis-à-vis him as his wife Alice, while also defining his own position in the romance as traditionally female.[28] Another stage routine was even more brazen in its innuendo, which, once again, employs heterocentrist conventions in order to position gay men as both the rivals of, and the substitutes for, straight women. In it Jack mentions Phil's latest film, *Wabash Avenue.* When faced with Phil's vanity about being a great "lover" in the film, however, Jack sarcastically remarks, "Phil, if you're such a great leading man, how come at the end of the picture, Victor Mature wins out?" "He didn't win, Jackson, he lost," Phil asserts. "What are you talking about?" Jack asks. "He got Betty Grable." "I know," Phil replies, "but he wanted me!"[29]

The radio programs could also suggest a touch of butch gay ambiance as part of Jack and Phil's relationship. The "Alice's pants" show (April 19, 1942) mentioned earlier features jokes about Jack's picture being displayed in the men's room of the Brown Derby restaurant, as well as in the men's room of the drugstore Phil and Jack are in. Another show reveals that Phil's Christmas gift to Jack is a manhole cover, on which Jack inscribes "Home, Sweet Home" before hanging it on a wall. And a cigar is definitely not just a cigar when it relates to Phil and Jack. On one program, Phil greets Jack with a "Glad to see you, baby!" To which Jack remarks, "Phil, that's a cigar in my mouth, not a teething ring," after which he notices Phil is in "great shape," "tan and rugged." Then there is Phil's recollection of the time he was at an NBC party in full dress suit. He took a bow and ended up shoving a lit cigar down his throat. But the topper to these Freudian cigar jokes is perhaps one cast member's rebuttal to Jack's assertion he's "no softie": "Jack had a cigar in his mouth when he was 7 years old — but he didn't light it until he was 21!"

Benny's autobiography contains only one anecdote that concerns his show's queer ambiance. It is worth quoting at length as it reveals that the far-ranging network of gay connotation on the radio and television programs over the years was to some extent intentional:

> Once we did a television program in which the entire plot was built around Rochester pressuring me to give him a week off. When I finally did he went to visit a friend in Palm Springs. Then he happened to see an ad in the classified section in which I was advertising for a "capable, conscientious person to perform household duties." He was sure he had been fired. . . . Rochester told his troubles to Don Wilson and Dennis Day. They told him they would fix me. They would scare Miss Dooley so much that she wouldn't work for me and Rochester would get his old job back. Dennis Day put on a tight-fitting dress and a flowered hat. Dennis did a very good swish — even though he's a happily married heterosexual tenor with nine lovely children. Dennis pretended to be Denise, a French maid who had formerly worked for me. . . . "Monsieur Benny, he ees, how you say? — a lush, and when he becomes drunken, he becomes veree passionate and he chases anysing zat is young." . . . Just then Don Wilson entered. He was also in drag. He said he was Hilda Swenson. She had formerly worked for

me, too, and had been molested when I got drunk and could not control my insatiable lust.[30]

After matters are cleared up, Jack splits the household chores between Rochester and his new assistant, Miss Dooley. "There's only one thing, Rochester," Jack says, "you and Miss Dooley will have to flip a coin to see which one of you rubs me with baby oil."[31] Benny's concern to heterosexualize the real Dennis Day before he proceeds with an anecdote centered on passion, lust, cross-dressing, and baby-oil massages reveals that the female impersonation here, and references to it elsewhere on the program, was developed with specifically gay drag ("swish") associations in mind.

Three pages later in the autobiography, the term "swish" returns, this time in relation to Rochester and a boxing bit he does with Jack on a program that finds Jack training for a bout with archrival Fred Allen: "There was the sound of an arm swishing through the air. The crack of a gloved fist meeting a glass jaw. The thunk of a body hitting the floor. 'Boss, boss,' Rochester cried, 'git up, git up.' "[32] Besides Benny's use of "swishing" while describing boxing (a sport with strong erotic undertones), the connection of all this with Fred Allen associatively links it to a letter Allen wrote to Groucho Marx, which Benny quotes later: "i made a picture with jack benny. . . . when the picture came out, jack looked like a westmore dream. i looked like some fag caught in a revolving door at the sloane house."[33]

If the radio program's discourse of disempowered comic gayness and gay femininity as devalued "effeminacy" was most campily developed through Jack's relationships with Phil and the boy sopranos, then it was in Jack's relationship with Rochester that the program's text of gayness was most complexly and even poignantly articulated. In *Sambo: The Rise and Demise of an American Jester*, Joseph Boskin traces the development of the Jack-Rochester relationship in terms of how it plays out what Leslie Fiedler refers to as "the impossible mythos" of an erotic bond between dark men and white men.[34] Citing such literary examples as Jim and Huck, Queequeg and Ishmael, and Chingachgook and Natty Bumppo, Fiedler makes a compelling case for the consistent appearance of "an archetype" in American culture that represents what he considers a regressive and infantile desire for a physical yet "ultimately innocent" union between white men and men of color.[35]

Simultaneously bound up with and counterpoised to white men's sexual envy of black men, their horror of miscegenation, and their overall sense of guilt about black men's history,[36] as well as with white men's misogyny, "the impossible mythos" of interracial male eroticism finds a remarkable number of sites for expression in American popular and mass culture, beginning, perhaps, with nineteenth-century minstrel shows.[37] Besides featuring a rather obvious symbolic fusion of black and white men in the practice of blackface performance, by the 1840s these shows often featured white men in drag as well as blackface. While a number of these drag blackface performances were low comedy burlesque turns by men in outlandish costumes, many were serious female impersonations, by so-called prima donnas. These female impersonators became an entertainment vogue in the 1870s and 1880s, particularly one Francis Leon, whom a white male reviewer described as "more womanly in his by-play and mannerisms, than the most charming female imaginable."[38] Another critic reported, "Heaps of boys in my locality don't believe yet it's a man in spite of my saying it was," and going on to say, "Leon was enchanting enough . . . to make a fool of a man if he wasn't sure."[39]

From the minstrel shows to vaudeville to early talking pictures, through performers such as Al Jolson, the tradition of blackface performance continued, as did cultural traditions that conflated blackness and feminine gayness or effeminacy through performances like these. Even a brief examination of popular culture from the 1850s to the time of the Jack-Rochester pairing in the 1930s reveals many moments in theater, film, and radio that can be read as expressions of "the impossible mythos" of the erotic union of white men and men of color. For the present, however, I will use the Al Jolson film *Big Boy* as my representative example.[40] In this film Jolson plays (in blackface) Gus, the loyal stablehand to an aristocratic Southern family. Early scenes depict Jolson's character attempting to deal with a hypermacho white bully. In one scene, Gus, disguised as a large sunflower, hits the bully's assistant in the head. The assistant lets out a piercing falsetto squeak as he drops his gun and falls to the ground. "Why, he's a pansy!" exclaims Gus. But Jolson's black character also proves to be a "pansy," with a white object of desire.

After being framed by the family's racing rivals, Gus is fired and proceeds to get a job as a waiter. While waiting on young Mr. Joe, a friend of his former employers, Gus gets caught up in a graphic description of how he would like to ride Big Boy to victory in an upcoming race: "Come on, Big Boy. You don't need the whip! Ride him, Big Boy. Ride him!" Gus gets so carried away enacting the race that he finally grabs the ears of a man seated nearby. "Excuse me, sir," Gus apologizes. "I thought you were a horse!" Soon after this, Gus attempts to serve a plate of oysters to a man and a suited woman with short slicked-back hair. "Listen, one of you boys ordered oysters. Which one was it?" Gus asks. "That's not a he, that's a she!" the man at the table shouts over a close-up of the lesbian nervously smoothing back her hair—to which he adds scornfully, "What's the matter with you, can't you tell?" "Lately, I ain't so good," is Gus's reply. After more bickering about the order, Gus turns to the man and says, "You're going to eat those oysters, if I have to sleep with you!" Rejected one final time, Gus takes the oysters, now with their inter- and extratextual associations with queerness and male potency, over to Mr. Joe, who is sitting at a table that has a vase of daisies on it, looking just like miniature sunflowers. The ensuing action at the restaurant, involving a French song performed by Gus, replete with suggestive hand gestures; Gus's brandishing of a large knife while threatening to cut off a man's nose; and a blackout that finds Gus and Mr. Joe hiding under a tablecloth, develops the interracial gay text of the suggestively titled *Big Boy*.[41]

The domestic or pseudo-domestic context for the erotics of black and white male relations often found in American cultural texts was perhaps most thoroughly articulated in our century through certain Jack Benny radio and television programs concerning Jack and Rochester's interaction as latter-day Robinson Crusoe and Friday.[42] The one *TV Guide* article written about actor Eddie Anderson is, in fact, titled "Jack Benny's Man 'Rochester.' "[43] Actually, during the course of the television series Jack and Rochester's relationship became physically and emotionally closer and more complicated. On the radio series, Rochester's appearances were often limited to making telephone calls from home that interrupted Jack at his radio studio workplace. With its visually exploitable settings, Jack and Rochester's domestic space became more and more prominent on the television show. Soon many episodes of the Benny program came to resemble other television domestic sitcoms, with the major parts played out by Jack and Rochester.

Boskin's book offers a generally incisive overview of the development and the dimensions of their relationship. This material does have its problems, however, because although Boskin concludes that Jack and Rochester "forged an intimate coupling" during the radio and television series, he also seems intent upon making a homophobic case for what he calls the pair's asexual, interracial "odd couple purity" as opposed to their being branded by what he terms "the stigma of gayness."[44] Ironically, in tracing out Jack and Rochester's "odd couple purity," Boskin provides the material for a more gay-positive reading of the pair as a couple, albeit a traditional couple within straight models. For example, at one point, Boskin describes their relationship as one in which two men ultimately become "surrogate spouses," but where elements of "role reversal" also become highly articulated.[45] That is, Jack and Rochester become both "husband" and "wife" to each other: for every time Rochester does something like nursing Jack back to health, for example, the program has Jack doing something similar for Rochester. And, more generally, while Rochester is the one who performs most of the domestic duties while Jack earns a salary as a performer, it is Rochester who is the more "butch" of the two, with his low, gravelly voice and his penchant for gambling, nightspots, and an occasional street fight.[46]

One of Boskin's examples from a radio show bears repeating, for it reveals the degree to which the Jack-Rochester relationship often comes close to the "cutting edge," as Boskin himself puts it, as it engages issues of race and gayness. On the May 3, 1944, program, Jack feels he needs to rehearse the romantic scenes of his upcoming movie. He asks Rochester to help him by taking the woman's role. " 'Oh, Connie,' says [Jack] to Rochester, who has taken the part of Ann Sheridan, 'you've made me the happiest . . . ' " At this point, Mary Livingstone walks in, and deadpans, " 'Hello, Jack, what's Rochester doing on your lap?' 'Huh?' [Jack] answers, as if unaware of the situation. 'It's quite all right, Miss Livingstone,' Rochester assures her, 'he just asked me to marry him.' " And even though the action is quickly clarified for Mary, Rochester insists on playfully staying in his role, sweetly responding "Yes, Bill" to Jack's request that he start getting his clothes ready.[47] Although the race, gender, and sexuality politics of this scene are complicated and troubling, as black, working-class Rochester is positioned as a substitute for a white female movie star playing a wife-to-be, the suggestion of interracial erotics that developed from repeated moments like this in *The Jack Benny Program* marked out a space in radio and television that no other show at the time (or since) dared enter. Only a few years earlier, Boskin notes, a similar scene ended almost before it began when both Jack and Rochester expressed some discomfort at acting romantic with each other.[48]

From the mid-1940s on, Jack and Rochester's relationship as a couple worked itself out within the complicated comic and dramatic narrative tensions created when the program's generally conservative

comic containment of blackness, gayness, and the feminine was combined with elements of domestic sitcom parody, or combined with moments of interracial male erotic tenderness. Benny's description of the
changes in Rochester's role on the program in relation to Jack illustrates and summarizes the problems and the audacity of their union:

> Rochester appeared more often on my radio and television shows than
> any other single character. He became more than a butler. He was my
> housekeeper. He did the shopping and fixed the meals. He washed the
> dishes, vacuumed the rugs, waxed the floors and made the beds. He
> did the laundry. . . . Rochester drove the Maxwell. He drew my bath
> and when I was immersed therein, he handed me my soap, washrag
> and celluloid duck. Afterwards, he massaged me with baby oil. When
> I suffered a spell of insomnia, Rochester switched on the motor that
> gently rocked my bed and he sang, "Rock-a-bye, baby, in the
> treetop," until I fell asleep.[49]

After years of establishing this domestic, marital, and parental relationship on radio and television, when Jack asks Jimmy Stewart and
his wife to come to dinner at "our house" on one episode, it is supposed to be clear to everyone that Jack means his and Rochester's
house.

Boskin also cites many examples of Rochester's teasing tenderness, focusing on scenes in which Rochester puts Jack to bed, dresses
him, or helps to give him a bath. Whether singing a revised version of
"You Must Have Been a Beautiful Baby" as he tucks Jack into bed or
exclaiming "Love that man!" in the face of one of Jack's cute idiosyn-
crasies, Rochester often reveals a strong emotional bond to Jack that
complicates readings of their relationship that are only based upon the
oppressive race and power dynamics suggested by his position as
Jack's employee. But the gay suggestiveness of Jack and Rochester's
relationship is blunted because most of their tender moments place
their "impossible" interracial erotics within the regressive and infantile male phantasmic suggested by Fiedler, with Rochester as mother
(or mammy) and Jack as baby.

But not everything about Jack and Rochester's expression of emotion for each other on Jack Benny programs can be neatly classified
(and perhaps dismissed) as the product of an infantilized, regressive,
or racist male desire for other men. One of the most often cited scenes
involving Jack and Rochester has nothing to do with Rochester's out-
smarting Jack, or Jack's demanding Rochester do demeaning chores,
or with Rochester and Jack being placed in such mock-heterosexual

domestic roles as husband-wife or mother-child. The moment occurs at the end of a 1953 television program set on New Year's Eve. As critic Gibert Seldes describes the show:

> Benny played a beautiful role—the man who was so sure of himself that he has not made a date for New Year's Eve and then watches one group after another drift away from him, finds himself rejected by those he knows, shouldered out of the way by strangers he tries to join, and then, utterly forlorn, goes home, but tries for a moment to brazen it out before Rochester (who is infinitely more resplendent, in white tie and tails, than his employer, and is moreover about to start out jubilantly for what promises to be the best party in the world). Rochester sees through the deception, and one of the most touching comedy scenes ever done in television follows: the two men sit down together and drink champagne and talk to each other. There were "social values" outside the range of comedy there, too, but they could not have existed if the characters had not been so soundly and solidly created before us.[50]

Benny's memories of this crucial episode are tellingly preceded by the material quoted earlier in this chapter about his character's being a "bachelor," Mary Livingstone's "heckler-secretary" character, and Jack's general lack of success with women. "There's a kind of bitter-sweet side to the sex game," Benny continues, "and if you play it somewhere between broad farce on the one hand and tragedy on the other, you get a fine irony which reflects a true-to-life situation."[51] In this context, Benny's subsequent retelling of the New Year's Eve episode that ends with Jack and Rochester celebrating the holiday together becomes the illustration of how the series dealt with the "bittersweet side to the sex game." As if simultaneously to point up and to deny Rochester's position as a romantic and domestic partner in this episode, and throughout *The Jack Benny Program*, Benny follows his description of the show with "Thanks to my wonderful wife, the real-life Jack Benny was never lonely on New Year's Eve."[52] On many of the television shows you can spot a wedding band on Rochester's finger, even though, narratively, he remains single. Likewise, many shows reveal Jack sporting a pinky ring, a favorite accessory of some gay men. I like to think they gave them to each other.

CHAPTER FIVE

The Sissy Boy, the Fat Ladies, and the Dykes

Queerness and/as Gender in Pee-wee's World

In all the things I've read or heard about Pee-wee Herman, his shows, and his films, only two commentators even begin to consider the specifically queer gender dynamics centered around Pee-wee/Paul Reubens. Bryan Bruce, in "Pee Wee Herman: The Homosexual Subtext," is right on target when he says, "The most exciting aspect of Pee Wee Herman, so far, remains his role as vindicator of the sissies," adding elsewhere that Pee-wee tends to "undercut masculinity . . . by feminizing it."[1] "The Mail-Lady," the first section of Ian Balfour's "The Playhouse of the Signifier: Reading Pee-wee Herman," toys with, but never directly engages, the idea that Pee-wee's gay sexuality (and the queerness of other characters) might be spoken through gender. Consider this pair of quotations, which follow each other early in the article:

> For Pee-wee's mail man is a "mail-lady," a phrase that—given the overdeterminations encoded by the sexual hijinks on the show—takes on an added resonance: the *male*-lady. And, indeed, the phrase the "mail-lady" can be switched into its converse, the lady-male, faster than one can change channels by remote.
>
> It doesn't take very long to recognize the gay subtext, intertext, or just plain text of the Pee-wee episodes, most clearly legible in the figure of Jambi, the drag queen genie adorned with a turban, flaming red lipstick, and a single earring.[2]

Here and elsewhere, Balfour is on the verge of linking the show's gender destabilization with queerness (or is that linking the show's queerness to gender destabilization?), but he can't seem to bring himself to do it explicitly. To be fair, Balfour's reluctance probably arises from an attempt to avoid stereotypically aligning gayness with the feminine/effeminate and lesbianism with the masculine/butch. In any case, after the first page, the word "gay" is dropped, and the "Mail-Lady" section opts for the suggestive, innuendolike approach to speaking homosexuality through heterocentrist notions of cross-gender identification that Balfour seems to wish to avoid:

> He [Pee-wee] then perks up to advise the boys and girls that next time he will tell the story of the "part-time boy." The part-time boy is, of course, Pee-wee: and this phrase too has to be understood in more than one sense. Part-time *boy*, because Pee-wee is part-time boy and part-time girl, if only in his most hysterical and histrionic moments. But also *part-time* boy because the other part of the time Pee-wee is something like a man.[3]

Without a specifically gay cultural-historical context to clarify things here, Balfour's parallel between Pee-wee as a "hysterical and histrionic" girl and Pee-wee as "*something like* a man" can only be read as a reiteration of two heterosexist standards about gay men: (1) they are screaming queens/woman wannabes, and (2) they are less than/something other than "real" (read: heterosexual) men. Given this, it's no surprise that the only appearance of the word "gay" in the article is connected to Jambi ("the drag queen genie") and men wearing lipstick ("Jambi . . . is one of the few male characters on television to wear lipstick, and Pee-wee may be the only other one").[4]

Having said this, I still think Balfour's initially suggestive juxtaposition of gender (mail-lady/lady-male) and (homo)sexuality (implicitly lesbian/more explictly gay) is an important one to work with in discussing Pee-wee and his texts. I will carry out this discussion within a particular queer context: that of the feminine gay man. Even more specifically, this reading of Pee-wee and his texts will be influenced by the positions of, and discourses surrounding, feminine gay men and boys growing up in white, heterosexual America in the 1950s and 1960s—a cultural and historical heritage Paul Reubens and thousands of gay men share.[5]

In this light, Pee-wee's queerness needs to be analyzed in relation to the then-popular understanding of homosexuality as always a case of gender inversion, where gender is patriarchally heterosexualized and the gay or lesbian is put in the cultural position of a substitute for (and an inferior imitation of) the opposite gender. Connected to this position is the cultural reinforcement of rigid gender roles that subordinated everything considered "womanly" and "feminine." But it is also important to recall that the articulation of Pee-wee's gender position as a sissy gay within 1950s and 1960s discourses is mediated by, and negotiated within, queer gender discourses of the 1980s and 1990s.[6] That is, in Pee-wee's world gender is often reconceptualized through queerness as much as queerness is expressed through traditional straight cross-gender positions.

In "The Cabinet of Dr. Pee-wee: Consumerism and Sexual Terror," Constance Penley points out that "the periods, styles and objects [of *Pee-wee's Playhouse*] are, of course, not arbitrarily chosen: they have been selected for parodic recycling because they have their origins in what must have been the childhood and adolescence of the 'real' Pee-wee Herman, the thirty-five-year-old Paul Reubens."[7] I would add to this that the attitudes to gender and sexuality (and the relationship between the two) that Pee-wee and his texts express also "have their origins in what must have been the childhood and adolescence" of Reubens. The popular press has often called Pee-wee "thirty-five (or so) going on ten," and it is within this complex and often contradictory attempt to work alternately or simultaneously with(in) the past (childhood; the 1950s and 1960s; pre-Stonewall) and the present (adulthood; the 1980s and 1990s; post-Stonewall) that Reubens, through Pee-wee, expresses his "sissy boy" and feminine gay worldview. Given this postmodern time warp, it is often difficult to form clear-cut political readings for Reubens's queer deployment of gender in Pee-wee's universe. Frequently the most conventional codes of queerness as heterosexualized cross-gender identification will be juxtaposed or will coexist with more progressive queer reworkings of the masculine and the feminine.[8]

Of course, the possibility of reading the Pee-wee texts' presentation of queerness and/as gender in a camp register makes coming to an ideological bottom line even trickier. Penley finds that Reubens is relatively evenhanded in his uses of camp in order to have "subversive fun" with gender and sexuality: if Miss Yvonne becomes "the Burlesque Queen of camp theatre, her femininity exaggerated into a parody of itself," then Pee-wee's feminine gay persona is campily coded through his "mincing step, affected gestures, exaggerated speech, obvious makeup and extreme fastidiousness."[9] If this is the case, then camp's impulse to "satirize and celebrate," which Penley points out, might bring us to wonder just what about gender and sexuality is being satirized or celebrated in Pee-wee's world—and why. If Miss Yvonne's character is a parody of a caricature, is Pee-wee's "mincing" fag the same? Or are they both celebrations of these (stereo)types? Perhaps the answer to these questions depends upon the gender and sexuality agendas of the camp reader, as well as the particular example of camp she/he is faced with. For example, I find it difficult to read Miss Yvonne's camp parody of conventional 1950s-1960s femininity in exactly the same way I interpret Pee-wee's campy comment on the codes of feminine gayness. While both satirize popular notions of gender and sexuality, Pee-wee's character also seems to function for many queer viewers as an affirmation of the look, behavior, and attitude of the feminine gay.

In "The Incredible Shrinking He[r]man: Male Regression, the Male Body, and Film," Tania Modleski places Pee-wee's camp within the context of postmodernism—and then condemns both camp and postmodernism for their attempts "to escape accountability by relying on the alibi of the figurative—indeed on the alibi of the alibi: nothing is what it seems or where it seems; nothing is taken seriously."[10] Relating all this to our culture's tradition of regressive male "escapist fantasy—even if its function is to serve as a cover story for a hidden gay text," Modleski finds that "insofar as Pee-wee can 'become woman' and at the same time revile through comic exaggeration the very traits that constitute 'womanliness,' he reveals how the desire to appropriate and the need to denigrate can easily coexist in male attitudes towards femininity."[11] In first separating, then conflating, straight men and gay men in this section of her essay, Modleski does her otherwise provocative argument (as well as gay men) a disservice. Men may have misogyny in common, but gay men's misogyny, particularly that of feminine gay men, needs to be discussed with more attention to its specific psychological and cultural foundations and patterns.

Besides, as a gay character, Pee-wee less "becomes woman" than represents an expression of gay femininity, less "reviles . . . womanliness" as some sort of essential category than reviles traditional attitudes toward its cultural constructions and surfaces. In saying this, I don't want to suggest that all instances of gender representation and gender play in Pee-wee's world are free of misogyny. Nor do I want to suggest that because certain forms of gay misogyny might have different social and psychological roots than the misogyny of straight men, it is any more excusable.[12] What I do want to call for here in relation to the issue of misogyny in Pee-wee texts, and in other forms of gay camp (including drag/female impersonation), is a more careful consideration of the particular gay contexts in which this camp (postmodern or not) is produced, as well as the possibility of variant audience readings of these particular texts' uses of camp in relation to gender and sexuality.[13]

But aside from Bryan Bruce's article, most academic and popular writing about Pee-wee Herman has foregrounded gender concerns in a heterocentrist manner. That is, these articles implicitly set up straight men and straight women as the ultimate reference points for their analysis of gender because their authors don't seriously consider the possibility that the gayness, lesbianism, and bisexuality in Pee-wee's image and texts might be crucial to that destabilization of gender roles they're all so excited about. If anything, it is the queer tone and context of Pee-wee and his world that allow for, and encourage, most of the gender confusion and reconceptualization. When homosexuality does enter the discussion in these articles, it is usually in the form of questioning, or being suggestively vague about, Pee-wee's *exact* sexual orientation (anything to keep from acknowledging he is fundamentally a gay boy-man), or of acknowledging the character's and a text's gayness at one point only to render explicit gayness invisible again at another (the Balfour article), or to downplay its importance (the Penley article: "Perhaps too much has been made of the homosexual subtext in *Pee-wee's Playhouse*").[14] Investigating how differences in sexualities are culturally gendered from childhood, and how, therefore, the gender play in Pee-wee's world is inextricably bound up in the play of queerness across its characters and texts seems not to be on most commentators' critical agendas.[15]

To return to an earlier point for the moment, while the Playhouse, its inhabitants, and its visitors attempt to recreate a 1950s-1960s sissy boy's perceptions and fantasies, we can't forget that Pee-wee is the 1980s creation of an adult gay man, Paul Reubens. This being the case, Pee-wee and other Reubens creations might also be considered against the backdrop of queer attitudes, politics, and styles that developed between the 1950s and the 1980s. As a feminine gay, Reubens might decide to have lots of athletic, traditionally masculine-looking men as Pee-wee's "friends": Tito, the lifeguard; Cowboy Curtis; Ricardo, the soccer player; Mickey, the weightlifting escaped convict; Captain Carl, the ship's skipper; a Marine Corps chorus.[16] But if these men are coded as (stereo)typically butch in an "old-fashioned" gay way, they are simultaneously presented as soft and pretty (as gay "boy toys" or boyfriends).[17] And while many of these men are erotically displayed as ethnic exotics, and therefore as regressively racist examples of "forbidden" sexual desires, when they speak and interact with Pee-wee they seem as friendly and familiar as the multiracial cast of men on *Sesame Street*.

Pee-wee's 1950s sissy boy can't, however, take direct erotic notice of these butch-looking men; so, as many feminine gay viewers have done (or have felt culturally compelled to do), he usually expresses his desire for them by using women as his erotic representatives. To this end, Reubens creates women characters—Miss Yvonne, especially, but also Mrs. Rene, Mrs. Steve, and Winnie the schoolteacher in *Big Top Pee-wee*—who can verbalize and act out Pee-wee's desires.[18] Yet these women are (stereo)typed by certain excesses, which might be explained as part of an overdetermined coding of Pee-wee's/Reubens's hidden and projected gay desires. These marks of excess could also be the result of a sissy boy's/feminine gay man's love-hate relationship with the gender he recognizes his affinities with even while he feels restricted by conventional straight definitions of that gender. Reubens/Pee-wee is the sissy boy/feminine gay man who both enjoys and resents his connection with women. This position is even more intensely held for having been developed in a period such as the 1950s and the 1960s in the United States, when gender was rigidly heterosexualized and publicly defined in a manner that attempted to keep women second-class citizens.

The sissy boy/feminine gay man knows he's not like men, not "masculine," in the way it is defined by straight patriarchal culture. But to be told by that same culture that he is, therefore, like a woman, is heterosexually "feminine" and that he functions as a woman substitute or as an imitation woman isn't usually a welcomed or enviable alternative—although it often seems the only one, given the absence of homosexuality as a male/masculine choice. The resentment and dislike of women by which gay men—particularly feminine gay men—are (stereo)typically characterized by straight culture and even by much of queer culture, stem less from gay men's problems with actual women than from their problems with the heterocentrist and patriarchal cultural definitions and depictions of women forced upon them. For this reason alone, the "one-size-fits-all" approach to male misogyny that Modleski and others employ when critiquing Paul Reubens's work with women characters is not very sensitive to how the particular position of gay men within patriarchy has been constructed in relation to concepts of "woman" and the "feminine." Certain things Reubens does with women characters might be misogynistic, but, as mentioned earlier, we need to consider more carefully how these instances may express misogyny of a distinctly gay variety, with complicated psychological and cultural foundations of its own, perhaps more comparable to straight women's misogyny than to that of straight men.

So, in Pee-wee's world, Miss Yvonne has the "biggest [bouffant] hair" and is a vain hyper-1950s feminine type. Mrs. Steve and Mrs. Rene are food-obsessed and fat. The schoolteacher progresses from being an extra-nice and prim 1960s blonde girl-next-door to becoming the lover of an entire troupe of Italian acrobats who are brothers. But while these excessive women may express Pee-wee's/Reubens's gay desires (Miss Yvonne, Winnie, sometimes Mrs. Rene as man-eaters) or his sexual frustrations (Mrs. Rene, Mrs. Steve as overeaters), these women are not passive tokens of homosocial or erotic exchange between men. Their energy and aggressiveness parallel Pee-wee's hyperactivity, and they all stand in contrast to the rather bland pleasantness of the male sex objects on the show. These women are as much counterparts to, and examples for, the closeted Pee-wee as they are unwitting shills for him. For every moment when Pee-wee does something like cutting in on Miss Yvonne in order to dance with Tito, there is another like the one in which he watches Miss Yvonne intently as she seduces the Conky repairman (or some other hunk) with lines such as "Is that a wrench in your pocket?" and then provides the camera/audience with a sly, knowing, and approving look after Miss Yvonne has made a successful pickup.

At least some of these excessive women can also be read in specifically adult gay culture terms as one half of a classic team: feminine gay man and "fag hag," or, to use a more recent term, "fag moll" (although I prefer "women friends of gay men"). In its stereotypical form this pair consists of a thin, witty-bitchy, stylish man and a fat and/or flashily dressed and made-up woman, who often appears to be emulating the look of drag queens rather than that of conventional straight feminine glamour. Indeed, fag moll Mrs. Steve can be read as a drag queen — at least one commentator dubbed her "the Divine stand-in."[19] As fag molls, Mrs. Steve, Mrs. Rene, Miss Yvonne, and even the Cowntess often receive the cruel and bitchy end of Pee-wee's schtick, with fat jokes, vanity jokes, and sexual double entendres aplenty at their expense.[20] Even seeing Pee-wee as "one of the girls" doesn't help matters in these cases — it only makes certain moments on the television shows and specials seem like queer remakes of *The Women*, with a different feminine gay man (Paul Reubens rather than George Cukor or R. W. Fassbinder) directing as well as participating in the action.[21]

For balance and counterpoint, however, there are many examples of Pee-wee's camaraderie with women characters, including suggestions that Mrs. Rene and Miss Yvonne on the television series and Simone the waitress in *Pee-wee's Big Adventure* serve as Pee-wee's female doubles, representing parallels to his gay femininity — as when Pee-wee gives his wish to Miss Yvonne (on *The Pee-wee Herman Show*) by asking Jambi to make Captain Carl "really like her," or when Pee-wee leaves Mrs. Rene in charge of the Playhouse when he goes "camping" with Cowboy Curtis, or when Pee-wee and Simone sit in the head of a large model dinosaur, share their dreams, and realize they are soulmates.[22] These and other examples of Pee-wee and women characters bonding and doubling are generally worked out as moments of gay femininity connecting with straight femininity rather than as moments in which heterocentrist notions of gayness as an imitation of straight femaleness are being evoked. The much-cited episode in which Pee-wee plays Miss Yvonne on a practice date with Cowboy Curtis stands as an excellent illustration of the type of straight cross-gender positioning Pee-wee usually refuses to accept. Initially reluctant to substitute for Miss Yvonne in a date rehearsal staged by the Cowntess, Pee-wee reluctantly gives in, but remains uncomfortable until he begins a camp parody of the traditional straight female position. When the Cowntess urges Curtis to kiss Pee-wee for the grand finale, Pee-wee stops the proceedings. While it is possible to read this scene as an (unsuccessful) attempt to establish Pee-wee's heterosexual credentials, seen queerly this moment reveals that gay Pee-wee doesn't want to be seen or used as a substitute for a straight woman: he may be *like* Miss Yvonne in many ways (being attracted to Cowboy Curtis is only one of them), but he isn't Miss Yvonne.

While Modleski is concerned about how other articles on Pee-wee implicitly treat his lack of interest in girls as examples of the old idea that "homosexuality is a result of arrested development and involv[es] man's turning away from the 'mature' object choice, woman," she proceeds to argue her points in a heterocentrist manner.[23] Modleski's ultimate criticism seems not to be that the statements about Pee-wee's being uninterested in or "grossed out" by girls-women might be homophobic, but that Pee-wee's rejection of girls-women is let off the hook with only "lighthearted" commentary. Finally, Modleski condemns Pee-wee along with all other little boy-men: "this dismissive attitude . . . is congruent with the misogyny of patriarchal ideology and reveals a contempt for females Freud saw as characteristic of 'normal' masculinity."[24] From this position, it might not occur to

Modleski to question and more carefully examine the heterocentrist assumptions behind assertions in the articles she critiques that Pee-wee "is . . . another sort of boy, one who simply isn't interested in girls."[25] It is one thing to say Pee-wee isn't romantically or sexually interested in girls-women (or that he rejects them on these counts); it is quite another to have this represent a general rejection and dismissal of women.

But this is just what is done in Modleski's critical discussion of Pee-wee, as much as in the work of others she cites (Balfour, Penley). As a sissy boy/feminine gay man, Pee-wee might not be sexually interested in girls-women, but he is certainly very interested in them in many other ways that cannot be called "dismissive" or "misogynistic"—he's interested in them as friends. To briefly bring in the example of a similar heterocentrist take on another Playhouse character, Balfour argues that there is one "exceptional moment" on the series in which Jambi seems to become "the stereotypical masculinist male." This is when "against all expectations, Jambi chooses to have a female genie head as his companion."[26] Given Jambi's character as feminine gay, this moment is hardly atypical: Jambi wishes to have a girl friend, not a girlfriend. With their fixation on sex as the primary bond between men and women, heterocentrist positions and readings constantly attempt to recast the relationships (real and representational) between women and gay men in terms of sexual antagonism. By these terms, gay men hate and dismiss women because they don't want to have sex with them, or jealously want to be women, or covet their men.

Besides his straight women friends, another group of women important to defining Pee-wee's sissy boy/feminine gay position, as well as central to establishing the general queerness of Pee-wee's world, are the tomboys/dykes. Not surprisingly, this group has been almost totally unacknowledged in discussions of Pee-wee Herman texts. Aside from John Goss's short film "*Out*"takes (1990, which "outs" Dixie as a dyke), and the occasional informal conversation, lesbians seem to be invisible to most people looking at Pee-wee's television shows and the films. Taken together, these dykes represent further illustration of the mediation between 1950s-1960s and 1980s-1990s styles and attitudes typical of Reubens's work: the codes of butch-as-heterosexualized male and femme-as-heterosexualized female meet, and often mingle with, more queerly gendered looks, attitudes, and behaviors, including lesbian-butch and lesbian-femme. Often, dyke characters coded as butch are used as counterparts to Pee-wee's/

Reubens's feminine gay personality: Reba the mail-male lady, Dixie the cabdriver, Herman Hattie (*The Pee-wee Herman Show*), Large Marge (*Pee-wee's Big Adventure*), and k. d. lang (*Pee-wee's Play-house Christmas Special*).[27] Whether you read these butches as het-erosexually masculinized or queerly masculine often depends upon the episode, the scene, the moment, and the spectator.

Most often, however, the straight masculine codes of dress and be-havior connected with these butch dykes are combined with just enough androgynous or feminine coding to suggest that they operate in the space of some lesbian reconceptualizing of masculinity rather than as imitations of straight men. That is, they seem to be butches who are both woman-identified and masculine. In any case, it makes queer sense that Reba is in the Playhouse with Pee-wee when it becomes lost in space and enters an alternative universe in which Miss Yvonne's double appears as a bald alien. Or that when Reba and Dixie appear in dresses at one Playhouse party they elicit the same type of surprised comment as when Pee-wee gets out of his prissy plaid suit and red bow tie and into more butch attire (a baseball uni-form, a cowboy outfit). Or that Herman Hattie (note the first name), hoping to get a kiss, echoes Pee-wee's dialogue to Miss Yvonne, and will trust only Pee-wee to guard her jeep's tools and paraphernalia ("with your life"). Or that k. d. lang is the only guest star on the Christmas special who interacts with the entire Playhouse crew during a spirited rendition of "Jingle Bell Rock."

But there is another side to these suggestions of complementariness between sissy Pee-wee and the butch dykes. For if these dykes are depicted as Pee-wee's "opposite" queer gender comrades, they are also often presented as uncomprehending of the world of the feminine gay man, as well as incomprehensible within this world. Reba is con-stantly befuddled by what happens in the Playhouse (one time calling the Playhouse and its inhabitants "twisted"), Dixie is abrupt and un-communicative, k. d. lang tries too hard to fit in and appears awk-wardly hyperkinetic, Herman Hattie is a laughable hillbilly hick with a skunk stuck to her "butt," and Large Marge metamorphoses into a monster. But this ambivalent presentation of butches in Pee-wee's world accurately reflects queer cultural history, past and present, as it suggests the longstanding suspicion and distrust between lesbians and gays (particularly between butches and sissies), which has only recently begun to change in any significant way with the revival of queer coalition politics, particularly around AIDS and women's health issues.

If the femmes in Pee-wee's world are treated more benignly, it is perhaps because they seem less like "others" to the sissy boy—he has the expression of queerly reconfigured femininity in common with them. The only femme Pee-wee seems uncomfortable with is Sandra Bernhard, appearing in one episode as an operator who aggressively vamps Pee-wee over the picture phone. Bernhard's charade of straight femininity here (which parallels her off-screen "I'm not a lesbian" pronouncements at the time) causes Pee-wee great irritation, and he quickly cuts off her parodic seduction scene.[28] But Pee-wee can enthusiastically greet each cartoon featuring Penny, a femme tomboy who has interesting relationships with a mermaid, an imaginary twin sister, a real sister, and Dorothy Lamour, among other females; and he can have fun singing "Hey Good-Lookin' " with Dolly Parton during her visit to Pee-wee's Playhouse on an episode of her own variety series (that is, until he suspects her of getting romantic with him).

And then there is Miss Yvonne, the character who has been with Pee-wee since his nightclub beginnings—at once the hyperfeminine straight woman who expresses Pee-wee's gay desires, the fag moll, and the femme dyke. Miss Yvonne's position as (unwitting) femme lesbian is most clearly articulated in *The Pee-wee Herman Show* when Herman Hattie, the hillbilly butch in coonskin cap and buckskin, romances "Miss Y" by presenting her with a bottle of "Rocky Mountain Valley Violet Perfume." Later, in the beauty makeover episode of *Pee-wee's Playhouse*, Dixie asks Miss Yvonne if she could "do her" after she finishes with Mrs. Steve. But Miss Yvonne's queer textual status as femme isn't consistent, and seems a case of Reubens partially working out his feminine gayness through Miss Yvonne by connecting his cross-gender identification with her to queerness: so Miss Yvonne is the ultra-femme(inine) figure who lusts after the Playhouse hunks while occasionally being sexually paired through double entendres with butch dyke figures such as Dixie, Herman Hattie, and Reba.

If the queer readings offered thus far seem either tentative or tenuous, it is probably because the queerness of Pee-wee's world is understood by most viewers through connotation, as is the queerness in most mainstream cultural texts. D. A. Miller elucidates this in a discussion of Alfred Hitchcock's *Rope*:

> Now, defined in contrast to the immediate self-evidence (however on
> reflection deconstructible) of denotation, connotation will always
> manifest a certain semiotic insufficiency. . . . Connotation enjoys, or

suffers from, an abiding deniability. . . . *Rope* exploits the particular
aptitude of connotation for allowing homosexual meaning to be elided
even as it is also being elaborated. . . . In this sense, the cultural
work performed by *Rope*, toiling alongside other films . . . and other
cultural productions . . . consists in helping construct a homosexuality
held definitionally in suspense on no less than a question of its own
existence—and in helping to produce in the process homosexual
subjects doubtful of the validity and even the reality of their desire,
which *may only be, does not necessarily mean*, and all the rest.[29]

Substitute *Pee-wee's Playhouse, Pee-wee's Big Adventure, Big Top
Pee-wee*, and the other Pee-wee texts for *Rope* in the quotation above,
and Miller's observations about homosexuality as connotation will indicate both the pleasures and the painful limitations of Pee-wee's
world for queerly-positioned audiences. The air of insider, "wink-
wink," double-entendre queer cultural referentiality, linked to instances of more obvious queer cross-gender codes (but are they "obvious" only to certain queer readers?), has opened the space for my
analysis above. But the queer-deniability factor Miller refers to is
powerfully at work in Pee-wee's world, allowing for readings that
downplay queerness, separate it from other topics (most notably from
gender concerns), or render it invisible. Not surprisingly, this last
category of reading Pee-wee is the one favored in articles written for
mass-market newspapers and journals, which typically cast Pee-wee
as a wacky and disconcerting asexual or presexual man-boy who encourages outrageous and "naughty" behavior in similarly asexual or
presexual child viewers. It is a reading of his character and his work
that the closeted Reubens has encouraged in interviews conducted as
Pee-wee, while also coyly hinting at "offscreen" women admirers of
his character.[30] But one child viewer cited in Henry Jenkins, III,'s
article "Going Bonkers!: Children, Play, and Pee-wee" unwittingly
provided the best metaphor for the Pee-wee universe, as embodied in
his (in)famous Playhouse, when he called it a "crazy closet."[31] The
television Playhouse as "crazy" queer closet has its parallels in Pee-
wee's film house and farm, which offer similar self-contained, queer-
connotative environments set apart from the "normal" world (it makes
sense that in *Big Top Pee-wee* a stranded circus is quickly and easily
integrated into Pee-wee's farm).

Perhaps it is to be expected that Pee-wee and his friends are stuck
in a closet of queer representation-as-connotation, as most of Pee-
wee's world is constructed to fit into the conventions of children's
television and mainstream filmmaking, while it is also placed within

that time warp between the 1950s-1960s and the 1980s-1990s.[32] To make it even more difficult for Reubens to directly express queerness in his work, the 1980s-1990s seem to be shaping up as a period in which America is reworking the conservative ideologies of the 1950s-1960s. So Pee-wee's world is one in which safe sex is referred to, but only by way of the sight of Miss Yvonne quickly changing into a plastic raincoat and "a transparent plastic cap to protect her large, dome-shaped bouffant hairdo."[33] It is also a world where muscular men can be erotically displayed, but where Pee-wee can't even touch them—and where Dixie's demand that Miss Yvonne "do" her after doing Mrs. Steve can only result in a femme-inizing beauty makeover.

But there are closets within the closet of the Playhouse. In *Pee-wee's Big Adventure* there is the hidden and excessively guarded garage that houses Pee-wee's prized bicycle; *Pee-wee's Playhouse* contains a secret room that stores this same bike (and a bizarre monster helmet); the series and *The Pee-wee Herman Show* both feature the box containing Jambi, the queeny genie, a.k.a. "The Wish Man." Even *Big Top Pee-wee*, with its (albeit often parodic) heterosexual romance narrative has a closet-within-the-closet. Hidden behind a curtain in Pee-wee's top security experimental greenhouse is his most important project. Leading rugged circus manager Mace Montana (Kris Kristofferson) past oversized tomatoes and cantaloupes (on which Mace comments in deadpan double entendres), Pee-wee swears Mace to secrecy as he unveils his "hot dog tree." "You've got big ideas," Mace tells Pee-wee. Then, looking at the tree again, he comments, "I need one of those." "Help yourself, Mace!" exclaims Pee-wee. But if Pee-wee's (Play)house becomes, in many ways, a closet of and for queer connotation (with "secret words," double-entendre dialogue, campy bric-a-brac, and everything) and, as such, is the prison house of open queer expression, the closets-within-closets represent Pee-wee's desire to "come out" or "come forward." It is the desire of a closeted sissy boy to directly express himself in/to the outside world.

At the end of each episode of *Pee-wee's Playhouse*, Pee-wee pulls down the arm of a reproduction of the famous Greek discus-thrower statue, releasing his bike and "one-eyed monster" (slang for "penis") helmet. Once helmeted and on the bike, he bids his Playhouse pals and the audience good-bye before magically zooming out of a previously unseen boarded-up and padlocked door; he takes this route rather than going out by the front door, which is presided over by a reproduction of the Venus de Milo. So Pee-wee's "outing" of himself is provocatively presented here as a move from the "Venus de Milo" (the incomplete figure of desire) Playhouse door to the hidden "Greek discus thrower" door/space. That is, it is a move from a door that leads into and out of a place that indirectly expresses queerness (or expresses it strictly in cross-gender terms), to a place that indicates the potential for open, and even culturally sanctioned, gay identities and desires.

But the desire to be "out" (or to "come forward") and therefore to be is still expressed symbolically through the play of connotation, and even within these terms, coming out is cast as a dream, a fantasy, a wish. In *Pee-wee's Big Adventure*, Pee-wee wins the Tour de France and public acclaim with his unconventional (read: unathletic, unmasculine) biking style, but wakes up to find it was only a dream. Later in the film, his forays into the outside world on his bike end in humiliation (he falls off his bike in front of a group of boys) or disaster (his bike is stolen by another sissy boy who must sense its sexually symbolic importance).[34] Pee-wee's public reunion with his (homo)sexualized bike in this film is initially set to take place in the *basement* of the Alamo, which proves to be nonexistent in any case, as Pee-wee discovers to his mortification while his tour group laughs derisively. When he finally locates the bike, it is on a movie set, where he must cross-dress as a nun to get it back. And while Pee-wee may blast out of his fantastic Playhouse on his bike at the end of each episode, he always lands in an equally fantastic "outside" environment in the form of obvious back projections of the open road. The episode of *Pee-wee's Playhouse* where the secret word is "out" metaphorically translates the process of coming out into Pee-wee's developing an illness that makes his "emotions lie very close to the surface," as he tells Ricardo. But having come "very close" to blurting out these "emotions" to one of his love objects, Pee-wee retreats to his bed and soon feels "better." His bout of coming-out jitters passed, he is once again ready to take charge of his *implicitly* queer Playhouse-as-closet.

More and more it seems to me that Jambi, the queeny genie, might be the key to the closeted yet richly queer-connotative time-warp Zeitgeist of Pee-wee's world. As the deep-voiced drag diva hidden in a bejeweled box and the model for the coyly winking sphinx high atop the Playhouse, Jambi flamboyantly expresses a queer femininity that is both the "embarrassing" secret and the cause for celebration — in Pee-wee's world, and often in the straight and queer worlds outside. He is the fairy godmother who grants Pee-wee wishes (such as making him visible again after he has made himself vanish during a magic show), as well as being the (older gay generation?) voice of Pee-wee's conscience, often encouraging him to examine his motives and emotions before making a wish.

Connected as he is with effeminacy, queer femininity, drag culture, and magic and witchcraft, Jambi is a compelling and disturbing figure whose power and threat are contained because usually he can appear only at Pee-wee's behest (and only in the form of a head with no body, at that). As the most overtly queer character, Jambi and his magic powers must be carefully guarded, monitored by the regime of the closet of connotation that is Pee-wee's world. But, to quote D. A. Miller again, "if connotation . . . has the advantage of constructing an essentially insubstantial homosexuality, it has the corresponding inconvenience of tending to raise this ghost all over the place."[35] Locked away in his box most of the time, Jambi's queeny spirit still presides on the Playhouse roof as a campy sphinx—at once guarding the secret of Mondo Pee-wee's queerness while announcing it to the world at the beginning of each episode.[36]

Afterword

"You Flush It, I Flaunt It!"

This is being written a year after Paul Reubens was arrested for masturbating in an adult theater in Sarasota, Florida. But the summer of 1992 also marked Paul Reubens's return to mass culture in two films: *Batman Returns* and *Buffy the Vampire Slayer*.[1] Or is it Pee-wee Herman's return? The hysterical popular press and mass-media responses to the Paul Reubens affair were well documented and critiqued in the months following the arrest.[2] What it all boiled down to was this: the queerness of Reubens's Pee-wee persona was (just barely) tolerated by straight culture as long as it remained connotative and unconnected to a sexual body. Why? Because Warner Brothers, CBS, the Disney corporation, Mattel, Toys "Я" Us, Kiddie City, and other big and little capitalist businesses were making lots of money from Pee-wee's difference. But once Reubens queered the deal by being sexual in public, his market value as Pee-wee was nil—particularly since two groups these businesses made much of their Pee-wee profits from were kids and queers. This became a lethal combination when pornography and masturbation were added to the public understanding of Pee-wee's world.

Of course, in private, most people already thought Pee-wee was sexually "strange," but this could remain the skeleton in the Playhouse closet as long as Reubens remained popular, profitable, and potentially asexual. After the arrest, however, kids + sex + Pee-wee equaled exactly what you might guess it would in this culture: a playground for homophobic fantasies. More than one commentator at the time pointed out that the general media and public treatment of straight men caught in sex "scandals"—Rob Lowe, Ted Kennedy— was far different from that accorded Reubens: "When videotapes of Rob Lowe screwing female minors surfaced, he was teased, yet, in no

97

time, was on an Academy Awards show singing a treacly duet with Snow White."[3] What was left for Reubens-as-Pee-wee, however, was a final walk-on appearance during the 1991 *MTV Music Awards* show, which garnered him a prolonged ovation but no job offers or even any press statements by celebrities about the cultural and industry homophobia that was working to destroy Reubens/Pee-wee. These few minutes were the equivalent of those "AIDS awareness" red ribbons many celebrities wear on awards shows. Applause for Reubens/Pee-wee was a way for people to show their hipness without committing themselves to doing much.

After the scandal broke, only *Pee-wee's Big Adventure* director Tim Burton offered Reubens work, signing him to the small but crucial part of the Penguin's father in *Batman Returns*. I don't know if this part, and other aspects of the film, were rewritten in light of the trials of Reubens-as-Pee-wee, but Burton conceives the Penguin's problematic relationship to straight capitalist patriarchy in a manner that invites comparisons to Reubens's misadventures. At many points, the Penguin's narrative in *Batman Returns* seems to be a metaphor for the homophobic post-arrest cultural reconceptualization of Pee-wee and his Playhouse, as well as an exposé of the role of cultural oppression and repression in the Reubens/Pee-wee scandal.

In the film's opening scenes, Reubens, cast as a cold aristocrat, rids himself of his hyperactive firstborn by dumping him into a stream that empties into a sewer. Raised by penguins who live there, the Penguin creates a campy underground world with the human and material castoffs of above-ground culture. But the Penguin has a certain defiant pride in his subterranean world: "You flush it, I flaunt it!" he yells at corporate bigshot Max Schreck, the richest and most influential person in Gotham City. While the Penguin reveals a longing to be reunited with his parents, and to gain the approval of the people of Gotham, he also suggests that his destructive attitude is a response to a culture that shuns and tries to rid itself of those "who were born a little different." Taking advantage of the Penguin's desire to be accepted, Schreck convinces him to leave his underground world and run for mayor, as he hopes to control the city through the Penguin. After an initial show of support, Gotham voters turn on the Penguin when, caught off-guard, he is overheard comparing the populace to stupid sheep. Following this rejection, the Penguin decides to avenge himself by first joining forces with Catwoman, and then by playing the "Pied Penguin" in order to lure the children of Gotham to their deaths in pools of industrial waste that factories have been dumping into the Penguin's domain.

The rejected, "different" child has grown up within a (sub)culture he has constructed from the detritus of mainstream culture. But he returns to demand respect from the parent culture. Seeming to attain this, but only because of corporate exploitation, he is hounded by the public and dumped by the capitalists the minute he reminds everyone of his difference from them by stepping outside of a role that supports and flatters the (straight) masses. His revenge? — "polluting" the children of Gotham by bringing them into his world. This is the Penguin-as-Pee-wee, made all the more interesting as it is Reubens himself, in the guise of straight patriarchy, who throws away his "monstrous" son/alter ego. But the denied, repressed, and displaced body of Pee-wee symbolically returns from the sewers in *Batman Returns* to wreak havoc on the culture that consigned him to that realm.

In *Buffy the Vampire Slayer*, it is Reubens who returns from the (career) grave, while Pee-wee is kept in a girl's gym locker. Eerily made up to resemble those long-haired, goateed mug shots featured in early stories about his arrest, Reubens plays the companion of head vampire Rutger Hauer. With his alternately innuendo-laden and bitchy dialogue, and his penchant for teenaged males, Reubens's vampire is clearly gay. Even his name sounds feminine: Amilyn. But, in at least one case, Amilyn's hickeylike bite seems less to victimize the receiver than to allow the teen to express his gay lust for a friend — a lust he had been joking about moments before.

To a great extent, however, *Buffy the Vampire Slayer* exploits cultural fears about open gay expression through its use of Amilyn and his "victims." As a result, being vampirized by Amilyn/Reubens can be read either as being encouraged to freely express your gay lust, or as being recruited into homosexuality. For the most part the film considers both positions uncritically as (comically?) horrifying. Enter high school cheerleader Buffy (Kristy Swanson), who is trained by a stranger named Merrick (Donald Sutherland) to save young manhood from this fate worse than death. Although she and the audience initially mistake Merrick for a "dirty old man," his straightness finally separates him from Amilyn and the other vampires. In this film, the straight "dirty old man" preying on teenaged girls becomes a myth; a gay man preying on teenaged boys, however, is a plague that must be stopped.

A straight patriarch grooms a straight woman to pit herself against a gay man in order to "save" straight men (particularly her boyfriend,

Pike, played here by *Beverly Hills 90210* heartthrob Luke Perry). This is what *Buffy the Vampire Slayer* finally appears to be about. But this conventional story of straightness versus queerness, especially of straight women versus gay men, also acknowledges the pervasiveness, and the allure, of queerness through its use of Reubens. Although cast as antagonistic, Buffy's and Amilyn's relationship is the affective center of the film. Both supervised by patriarchal figures, both interested in the same man (Perry), both witty and inventive, Buffy and Amilyn have more in common with each other than with anyone else. In this context, it really comes as no surprise that the inside of Buffy's gym locker is adorned with a picture of Pee-wee Herman, rather than, say, Luke Perry. Buffy may love Perry, but she identifies with Pee-wee.

Buffy's final confrontation with Amilyn is played out amid campy one-liners that simultaneously suggest the connections between Buffy and Amilyn (that is, between straight women and gay men) even while they work to separate the characters through misogyny and gay-baiting:

AMILYN: Admit it, Buffy, don't you sometimes feel less than fresh?

BUFFY: You look like you're having a bad hair day.

While Buffy is "allowed" by Hauer's vampire chief to drive a stake into Amilyn's heart, director Fran Rubel Kuzui allows Reubens to have a long, funny death scene, in which Amilyn twice seems to slip out of the frame and die, only to return, moaning and groaning, a few seconds later. Finally dropping into the small space between a stairway and a wall, Amilyn twitches a few more times and is still. All that remains is for Buffy to overcome Hauer and the rest of his vampire "family," with a little help from her boyfriend. Her mission accomplished, Buffy, the *Cosmo* (or is that *Sassy?*) postfeminist, clad in a frilly white formal and her boyfriend's black leather jacket, climbs behind Perry as he rides his motorcycle into the sunset. The straight couple has been reunited, and the straight world has once again been saved from the threat of queerness. As the credits roll, (rumored-to-be-dyke) journalist Liz Smith, playing a television reporter, speculates about who was responsible for the recent excitement: a biker gang? cultists? She doesn't seem to have a clue that it was something queer.

So the traditional narrative, which conventionally ends with the happy straight couple (albeit partially updated by having it consist of a sort-of feminist and a sort-of neobeatnik) riding into the sunset, is appended by a newscast that is inaccurate because it denies the queerness we know is part of the story. This newscast is an example of the kind of "inning" straight culture currently encourages as a way to combat increasing queer visibility, as this visibility threatens the illusion that everything is (or should be) straight.[4] The film fades to black after the newscast, and the credits continue to roll. But just when you think the story is over, and that straightness has been reestablished as the final word through the eradication or the denial of queerness, the credits are interrupted for a final shot of Amilyn, still twitching in his corner.

It is difficult to say for certain how this image is meant to be read: as a sign of renewed threat (Amilyn might become the monster in a sequel?) or as a sign of empowerment (queerness remains alive and kicking in spite of straight narrative and cultural machinations?). Perhaps a radical queer reading would combine both positions, finding empowerment in Amilyn's threatening in-your-face qualities for the straight world. So Reubens-as-Amilyn might be a vampire in the film, but maybe he's only a monster if you go along with straight cultural (reading) positions. However, placing Reubens-as-Amilyn's final image outside the narrative proper, and at the tail end of the film—that is, after most people have left the theater or hit the VCR stop button—blunts queer-affirmative readings of the film's uses of the character and the actor. The queerness they represent might be the last word, but it is being spoken to an empty (or near-empty) house. One might say the same things about Reubens-as-Pee-wee in this film, as his in-joke appearance via a photograph is constructed to offer only the most cautious sign of support, as it (re)places Pee-wee within the closet of Buffy's locker.

I have gone on about the personal and professional fate of Paul Reubens/Pee-wee Herman since *Pee-wee's Playhouse* because, in many ways, the combined spectacle of the arrest, the negative media and corporate response, the more positive op-ed pieces, the *MTV Music Awards* appearance, and the roles in *Batman Returns* and *Buffy the Vampire Slayer* represents the complicated position of queers and queerness in contemporary (mass) culture. This panorama of queerness intersecting capitalism, consumerism, the media, women's issues, notions of the subcultural/marginal, as well as (sub)cultural production and reading practices, in turn suggests important issues queers and queer mass culture studies might continue to (re)examine *through* mass culture. The basic issues are ones that gay and lesbian activists and academics have been discussing and debating for years: notions of identity and identity politics; the relationship of feminism and queer cultures/theories/politics; the relationship of lesbian identities and cultures to gay identities and cultures; the relationship of mainstream/dominant/capitalist culture to queer cultures; the relationship of bisexuality, transsexuality, and other queernesses to gay and lesbian identities and cultures; the intersections of gender, race/ethnicity, and class with queerness.

Even though these topics are nothing new, examining them in public with reference to mass culture is relatively new. And this work with mass culture is particularly exciting because queers are using mass culture as the bridge between the streets and the ivory tower. Recontextualized by and reconsidered through production, texts, and reception, queer praxis and queer theory have met on fruitful mass culture ground recently: the feminist-lesbian camp of Ulrike Ottinger's films; Sue-Ellen Case's critical writing; *Dry Kisses Only*; *Designing Women*'s "The Strange Case of Clarence and Anita" episode; Judith Butler's defense of gay drag in *Gender Trouble*; Richard Dyer's *Now You See It*; the anthologies *How Do I Look? Queer Film and Video*, *Inside/Out: Lesbian Theories, Gay Theories*, and *AIDS: Cultural Analysis/Cultural Activism*; Robin Wood's bisexual critical readings in *Hollywood from Vietnam to Reagan*; the verbal and print debates between straight feminists, gays, lesbians, bisexuals, and queers about *The Silence of the Lambs* and *Basic Instinct*; the discussions of queerness, race, and censorship surrounding Robert Mapplethorpe's photographs, the airing of *Tongues Untied* on PBS, *Looking for Langston*'s production, and various NEA grant decisions; British television's *Out on Tuesdays* series; John Greyson's camp activist videos; the *Video Against AIDS* collection; the return of political camp and drag via AIDS and women's health activism; and the reexamination of feminist positions on pornography in the face of gay, lesbian, and bisexual production and criticism.[5]

It is my hope that this book might be added to this list for suggesting ways in which queerly interpreting things such as television sitcoms, film genres, stars, authorship, and audiences can become important cultural and political work. Since the consumption, uses, and discussion of mass culture as queers still find us moving between being on the "inside" and the "outside" of straight culture's critical language, representational codes, and market practices, we are in a position to refuse, confuse, and redefine the terms by which mass culture is understood by the public and in the academy.

But working through mass culture in order to turn the simultaneously conservative and postmodern '70s and '80s into the queer '90s won't be easy. For the past two decades, Western culture has been either hip or cynical enough to allow for—and even to encourage—certain types of queerness: the postliberation "beyond stereotyping" of *In Living Color*'s "Men on . . . " sketches and *The Silence of the Lambs*'s serial killer; the titillating suggestiveness of many "homosocial" buddy films and television shows (the *Lethal Weapon* films, *Designing Women*, *Thelma and Louise*, *Fried Green Tomatoes*, *Bosom Buddies*); and, of course, the ever-popular connotatively constructed "asexual" closet queer (Anthony Bouvier on *Designing Women*, Pee-wee Herman, gunnery sergeant Alva Lucille Bricker on *Major Dad*).[6] Very few clearly marked queer characters and texts that don't fit into one of these categories appear in mass culture—at least not without a great deal of trouble. For example, it seemed a minor miracle that some Public Broadcasting stations decided to air Marlon Riggs's *Tongues Untied* in 1991, and broadcast an edited version of Isaac Julien's *Looking for Langston* in 1992, as both films explore gay African-American erotics and culture. But even middle-class, middlebrow assimilationist attempts to represent queerness as just like straightness have failed to find a secure place in mass culture, for the most part. The gay couples in *thirtysomething* and *Roseanne*, the lesbian couple in *Heartbeat*, Amanda Donohoe's bisexuality in *L.A. Law*, and the lesbian founders of Cicely, Alaska, in *Northern Exposure* were pretty much here today, gone tomorrow on television. The movies *Longtime Companion*, *Maurice*, and *The Lost Language of Cranes* remained in that mass culture twilight zone between mall multiplex and art house, or between network television and PBS.[7]

Straight culture's paradoxical rejection of queerness that is either too different or too similar might bring us back around to examining "in-between" mass culture examples, such as those that are at the center of this book: Jack Benny and Rochester, Busby Berkeley musical numbers, women-centered sitcoms, Pee-wee Herman, the films of Dorothy Arzner and George Cukor, *Gentlemen Prefer Blondes*, and so on. It is in the queerness that circulates rather widely (if not always openly) in mass culture that I find the most frustrating and hopeful ground for queer studies in and outside of the academy—frustrating because most of this mass culture queerness remains discursively, politically, and economically beneficial only to straights and straight culture, framed and understood as it still is largely through the languages, codes, and systems of capitalism, patriarchy, connotation, and heterocentrism.

Because of all this, we queers have become locked into ways of seeing ourselves in relation to mass culture that perpetuate our status as *sub*cultural, parasitic, self-oppressive hangers-on: alienated, yet grabbing for crumbs or crusts and wishfully making this into a whole meal. Have we been, and are we now, little better than collaborators in our own continued invisibility, oppression, and marginalization, if in no other ways than by financially supporting capitalist entertainment enterprises and then keeping our queer interpretations of mass culture to ourselves? Or by accepting the idea that our readings and uses of mass culture must always be supplemental or alternative to those of straight culture? Wouldn't it be more politically and personally beneficial to spend our time, energy, and money creating, supporting, and critically reading only openly queer cultural products?

But I suppose the idea of being "open" suggests what is finally at stake here. The hopefulness I feel in the face of the frustrating position outlined above hinges on the possibility that the increasing visibility and audibility of queers in relation to mass culture production and reception will gradually establish academic and nonacademic discourses to challenge and redefine those ways of seeing and using mass culture that now invoke mass culture queerness only to deny/dismiss/contain it in order to maintain straight culture's pleasures and profits. By publicly articulating our queer positions in and about mass culture, we reveal that capitalist cultural production need not exclusively and inevitably express straightness. If mass culture remains by, for, and about straight culture, it will be so through our silences, or by our continued acquiescence to such cultural paradigms as connotation, *sub*cultures, *sub*cultural studies, *sub*texting, the closet, and other heterocentrist ploys positioning straightness as the norm.[8] Indeed, the more the queerness in and of mass culture is explored, the more the notion that what is "mass" or "popular" is therefore "straight" will become a highly questionable given in cultural studies—and in culture generally, for that matter.

Notes

Introduction

1. It might be argued that many texts including visible, "denotative" lesbians, gays, and/or bisexuals (or other queers, like the killer in *The Silence of the Lambs*) aren't necessarily "queer texts," because the "queerness" here is often more about oppressing the queer than it is about expressing it/her/him.

2. D. A. Miller, "Anal *Rope*," *Representations* 32 (Fall 1990): 119.

3. Ibid.

4. Michael Warner, "From Queer to Eternity," *Voice Literary Supplement* 106 (June 1992): 19.

5. Teresa de Lauretis, "Queer Theory: Lesbian and Gay Sexualities, An Introduction," *differences* 3, no. 2 (1991): iii.

6. William Safire's syndicated "On Language" column recently described "queer" as "a self-mocking term taken up by militant homosexuals" ("That Weird Bizarre," *The New York Times*, rpt. *The Morning Call* [Allentown, Pa.], July 26, 1992, F8). While Safire's understanding of "queer" is derived from Queer Nation's brand of radical politics, his perception of it as "self-mocking" misunderstands the camp elements often involved in expressing queer militancy.

7. Interviewed in Steve Cosson, "Queer," OUT/LOOK 11 (Winter 1991): 16.

8. de Lauretis, "Queer Theory," iii.

9. See Judith Butler, *Gender Trouble* (New York and London: Routledge, 1990), and "Imitation and Gender Insubordination," *Inside/Out: Lesbian Theories, Gay Theories*, ed. Diana Fuss (New York and London: Routledge, 1991), 13–31; and Sue-Ellen Case, "Tracking the Vampire," *differences* 3, no. 2 (1991): 1–20.

10. de Lauretis, "Queer Theory," iii.

11. Alisa Solomon, "Breaking Out," *The Village Voice* 37, no. 26 (June 30, 1992): 29.

12. Carol A. Queen, "The Queer in Me," *Bi Any Other Name: Bisexual People Speak Out*, ed. Loraine Hutchins and Lani Kaahumanu (Boston: Alyson, 1991), 20.

13. Looking through this book, I realize I have given rather cursory attention to specifically bisexual positions. Since examining bisexuality seems crucial in many ways to theorizing nongay and nonlesbian queerness—indeed, some see bisexuality *as* queerness (see note 12 above and its textual reference)—I consider the absence in this book of any extended discussion of bisexuality and mass culture a major omis-

sion. For the present, however, I will suggest one approach mass culture theory and criticism might explore in considering bisexuality and queerness.

Used to anchor a lesbian reading of *Gentlemen Prefer Blondes* in the first chapter of this book, Lucie Arbuthnot and Gail Seneca's "Pre-Text and Text in *Gentlemen Prefer Blondes*," (*Film Reader* 5 [1982]: 14–23; rpt. in Patricia Erens, ed., *Issues in Feminist Film Criticism* [Bloomington and Indianapolis: Indiana University Press, 1990], 112–25) also provides ideas useful to constructing a far-ranging bisexual interpretation of mass culture. Their notion that *Gentlemen Prefer Blondes*'s "narrative of [heterosexual] romantic adventure" serves as "a mere pre-text" for many viewers, who foreground another ("more central") nonheterosexual text involving Marilyn Monroe/Lorelei and Jane Russell/Dorothy, suggests that the film text is potentially bisexual as it combines both opposite sex and a same sex narratives (16). From their feminist-lesbian position, Arbuthnot and Seneca see the opposite sex (the "heterosexual") romantic narrative as being "continually disrupted and undermined" by the women-bonding aspects of the text (16). But is this the case? Is *Gentlemen Prefer Blondes* necessarily a text in which women-bonding undermines straight patriarchy or where homosexuality subverts heterosexuality? Couldn't we see the two narratives as coexisting in the text, as supplementing each other? In this light, a film like *Gentlemen Prefer Blondes* could be said to construct bisexual main characters in a bisexual text, as well as to encourage bisexual (or queer) positions and pleasures in spectators.

Any number of mass culture texts are constructed within the "pre-text" and "text" terms Arbuthnot and Seneca set out. Indeed, a number of the examples I cite in this book fall within this paradigm, and could be discussed as bisexual texts: *The Golden Girls* and other "lesbian" sitcoms, male buddy films, and so on. Thus far, feminist, gay, and lesbian studies have read these texts largely in terms of how the "pre-text" of "compulsory heterosexuality" is disrupted or contradicted by the "text" of women-bonding or same-sex erotics. But these works are constructed to support interpretations that see same-sex and opposite-sex affectional or erotic narratives not as separate and in conflict with one another, but as combining to offer a range of possibilities that could be called "bisexual."

For a psychoanalytic approach to the "repressed bisexual tendencies" in traditional Western cultures and cultural texts, see Robin Wood's *Hollywood from Vietnam to Reagan* (New York: Columbia University Press, 1986), especially those chapters on horror films and horror auteurs.

1. There's Something Queer Here

1. Jean Genet, *Gay Sunshine Interviews*, ed. Winston Leyland (San Francisco: Gay Sunshine Press, 1978), 73.

2. Gretchen Phillips, "The Queer Song," performed by Two Nice Girls, *Chloe Likes Olivia* (Rough Trade Records, 1991). Lyrics quoted by permission.

3. Janice Radway, "Reception Study: Ethnography and the Problems of Dispersed Audiences and Nomadic Subjects," *Cultural Studies* 2, no. 3 (October 1988): 361.

4. Ibid., 366.

5. Stuart Hall's article "Encoding/Decoding" informs much of my general approach to queer cultural readings of mass culture. This important essay is in *Culture, Media, Language*, ed. Stuart Hall, Andrew Lowe, and Paul Willis (Birmingham: Center for Contemporary Cultural Studies, 1980), 128–38.

6. Adele Morrison as quoted in "Queer," Steve Cosson, *OUT/LOOK* 11 (Winter 1991): 21.

7. Although the ideas that comprise "straightness" and "heterosexuality" are actually flexible and changeable over time and across cultures, these concepts have been—and still are—generally understood within Western public discourses as rather clearly defined around rigid gender roles, exclusive opposite sex desires, and such social and ideological institutions as patriarchy, marriage, "legitimate" child-bearing and -rearing, and the nuclear, patrilineal family. And all of this has been/is placed in binary opposition to "homosexuality" or "queerness." However, if we consider the notion of "queerness" in relation to the terms of the still commonly evoked utopian binary of sexuality (with its implicit dynamics of heterosexual gender stability versus homosexual [cross-]gender instability), it becomes clear that queerness, not straightness, describes an enormous space of cultural production and reception. For it is *deviance* from the demands of strict straight/heterosexual paradigms (however they are defined in a given time and place) that most often defines and describes our sexualized and/or gendered pleasures and positions in relation to movies, television, videos, and popular music. Indeed, many so-called straight mass culture texts encourage "deviant" erotic and/or gendered responses and pleasures in straight viewers.

8. These thoughts about queer spaces in mass culture are most immediately indebted to Robin Wood's "Responsibilities of a Gay Film Critic," *Movies and Methods II*, ed. Bill Nichols (Berkeley: University of California Press, 1985), 649–60, and Marilyn R. Farwell's "Heterosexual Plots and Lesbian Subtexts: Toward a Theory of Lesbian Narrative Space," *Lesbian Texts and Contexts: Radical Revisions*, ed. Karla Jay and Joanne Glasgow (New York: New York University Press, 1990), 91–103. Concerned with the politics of film critics/theorists (Wood) and the creation of uniquely lesbian narrative spaces for characters in literature (Farwell), these articles lucidly combine academic theory with gay- and lesbian-specific cultural concerns to suggest how and where being gay or lesbian makes a difference in cultural production and reception.

9. bell hooks, "Choosing the Margins as a Space of Radical Openness," *Yearning: Race, Gender, and Cultural Politics* (Boston: South End Press, 1990), 153.

10. While I use the term "regression" here in relation to queerness and mass culture, I don't want to invoke conventional psychoanalytic and popular ideas about queerness as a permanently infantilized stage past which heterosexuals somehow progress.

11. In "On Becoming a Lesbian Reader," *Sweet Dreams: Sexuality, Gender and Popular Fiction*, ed. Susannah Radstone (London: Lawrence and Wishart, 1988), Alison Hennegan offers many incisive examples of the complex workings of gender in the construction of queer identities and cultural reading practices, as well as indicating the reciprocity between sexual identity formation and reading cultural texts. Speaking of her adolescence, Hennegan states: "That I turned to ancient Greece need come as no surprise. If there's one thing everyone knows about the Greeks it's that they were all That Way. . . . That women's own voices were virtually silent, bar a few precious scraps of lyric poetry and the occasional verbatim transcript from a court hearing, did not then worry me. What I was looking for were strong and passionate emotions which bound human beings to members of their own sex rather than to the other. That the bonds depicted existed primarily between men didn't matter. In part this was because I spent at least half my adolescence 'being male' inside my own

head: 'gender identity confusion' in today's terminology, or 'male identified,' but nei-
ther phrase is right or adequate. I never for one moment thought I was a man nor
wished to be. But somehow I had to find a way of thinking of myself which included
the possibility of desiring women. And those who desire women are men" (p. 170).

12. Sue-Ellen Case, "Tracking the Vampire," *differences* 3, no. 2 (Summer 1991): 2.

13. Ibid., 3.

14. Ibid., 8, 12.

15. Some gay men will prefer the terms "effeminate" or "woman-identified" where
I use "feminine" in this section, and throughout the text. I find the former term still
too closely connected to straight uses that simultaneously trivialize and trash women
and gay men, while the latter term might appear to place gay men in the position of
essentializing theoretical transsexuals. Where I use "effeminate" in this book, it
should be understood as describing culturally dictated heterosexist ideas about gays
and gender (which queers might also employ).

16. Although most of these performers have an international gay following, this
list is rather Anglo-American. To begin to expand it, one would add names like Zarah
Leander (Germany), Isa Miranda (Italy), Dolores del Rio, Maria Felix, Sara Montiel
(Latin America and Spain), and Josephine Baker (France). As is the case in the
United States and Great Britain, while some national and regional queer cultural
work has been done regarding (feminine) gays and women stars, much more needs to
be done. Television series cited in this section: *Designing Women* (1986–present,
CBS), *The Golden Girls* (1985–92, NBC), *Murphy Brown* (1989–present, CBS), *The
Mary Tyler Moore Show* (1970–77, CBS).

17. Among the work on women stars that concerns feminine gay reception (with
the "feminine" aspects usually implied) are: Parker Tyler, "Mother Superior of the
Faggots and Some Rival Queens," *Screening the Sexes: Homosexuality in the Movies*
(Garden City, N.Y.: Anchor Books, 1973), 1–15 [on Mae West]; Quentin Crisp,
"Stardom and Stars," *How to Go to the Movies* (New York: St. Martin's Press, 1989),
11–30; Gregg Howe, "On Identifying with Judy Garland" and "A Dozen Women We
Adore," *Gay Life*, ed. Eric E. Rofes (New York: Doubleday, 1986), 178–86; Seymour
Kleinberg, "Finer Clay: The World Eroticized," *Alienated Affections: Being Gay in
America* (New York: St. Martin's, 1980), 38–69; Michael Bronski, "Hollywood
Homo-sense," *Culture Clash: The Making of Gay Sensibility* (Boston: South End
Press, 1984), 134–43; Jack Smith, "The Perfect Filmic Appositeness of Maria Mon-
tez," *Film Culture* 27 (1962–1963): 28–32. I might also include critic John Simon's
Private Screenings (New York: Macmillan, 1967) on this list, for its Wildean bitchy-
witty critiques of stars such as Elizabeth Taylor, Barbra Streisand, Anna Karina, and
Monica Vitti, which are embedded in film reviews. Simon may be a self-declared
straight, but his style and sensibility, in this collection at least, are pure scathing
urban queen—which works itself out here, unfortunately, to include a heavy dose of
misogyny.

18. Julie Burchill, *Girls on Film* (New York: Pantheon Books, 1986), 109.

19. More work is being done in these areas all the time. Some of the more recent
essays include: Richard Fung, "Looking for My Penis: The Eroticized Asian in Gay
Porn Video," *How Do I Look? Queer Film and Video*, ed. Bad Object-Choices (Seattle: Bay Press, 1991), 145–60; Kobena Mercer, "Skin Head Sex Thing: Racial Differences and the Homoerotic," ibid., 169–210; Mark A. Reid, "The Photography of
Rotimi Fani-Kayode," *Wide Angle* 14, no. 2 (April 1992): 38–51; Essex Hemphill,

"*In Living Color*: Toms, Coons, Mammies, Faggots and Bucks," *Outweek* 78 (December 26, 1990): 32–40; Marlon Riggs, "Black Macho Revisited: Reflections on a Snap! Queen," *The Independent* 14, no. 3 (April 1991): 32–34; Manthia Diawara, "The Absent One: The Avant-Garde and the Black Imaginary in *Looking for Langston*," *Wide Angle* 13, nos. 3/4 (July-October 1991): 96–109; Anthony Thomas, "The House the Kids Built: The Gay Imprint on American Dance Music," OUT/LOOK 2, no. 1 (Summer 1989): 24–33; Jackie Goldsby, "What It Means to Be Colored Me," OUT/LOOK 3, no. 1 (Summer 1990): 8–17; Kobena Mercer and Isaac Julien, "Race, Sexual Politics and Black Masculinity: A Dossier," *Unwrapping Masculinity*, ed. Rowena Chapman and Jonathan Rutherford (London: Lawrence and Wishart, 1988), 97–164.

20. Judy Whitaker, "Hollywood Transformed," *Jump Cut* 24/25 (1981): 33. Gail Sausser's "Movie and T.V. Heart-Throbs" chapter of *Lesbian Etiquette* (Trumansburg, N.Y.: Crossing Press, 1986) offers another expression of lesbian reception practices, their connection to gender identity, and the evolution of both through time: "I loved romantic movies when I was a teenager. I unconsciously identified with all the heroes who got the girl. Since I came out, however, my identifications have changed. Now I yell, 'No, no, not him!' at the heroine and root for her female roommate. What a difference a decade (or two) makes" (p. 57).

21. Whitaker, "Hollywood," 34.

22. Films mentioned in this section: *Sylvia Scarlett* (1936, RKO, George Cukor), *Gentlemen Prefer Blondes* (1953, Twentieth Century-Fox, Howard Hawks), *Trapeze* (1956, United Artists, Carol Reed), *To Live and Die in L.A.* (1985, New Century, William Friedkin), *Internal Affairs* (1990, Paramount, Mike Figgis), *Thelma and Louise* (1991, MGM, Ridley Scott), *Scorpio Rising* (1962–63, Kenneth Anger), *Home Movies* (1972, Jan Oxenberg), *Women I Love* (1976, Barbara Hammer), *Loads* (1980, Curt McDowell).

When I say certain mainstream films elicit a "wider range of queer responses" than films made by, for, or about lesbians, gays, and bisexuals, I am not commenting upon the politics of these films or their reception, only about the multiplicity of queer responses. And while the lesbian and gay films listed here are much more direct and explicit about the sex in them being homo, the sexual politics of these films are not necessarily more progressive or radical than that of the mainstream films.

23. The strength of the Monroe-Lorelei/Russell-Dorothy pairing on and off screen was publicly acknowledged shortly after the film's release when, as a team, the two stars went through the ceremony of putting prints of their hands and feet in the forecourt of Grauman's Chinese Theatre in Hollywood.

24. Al LaValley, "The Great Escape," *American Film* 10, no. 6 (April 1985): 71.

25. Michael Musto, "Immaculate Connection," *Outweek* 90 (March 20, 1991): 35–36.

26. Ibid., 36.

27. In the revised edition of *The Hollywood Musical* (London: BFI/Macmillan, forthcoming), Jane Feuer has added a brief section focusing on MGM's Freed Unit and Judy Garland that suggests ways of developing gay readings of musicals with reference to both production and queer cultural contexts. Mentioned in Feuer's discussions, Richard Dyer's chapter "Judy Garland and Gay Men," in *Heavenly Bodies: Film Stars and Society* (New York: St. Martin's Press, 1986), 141–94, is an exem-

plary analysis of how and why queers and queer cultures read and, in certain ways, help to create star personas.

28. Films mentioned in this section: *The Pagan* (1929, MGM, W. S. Van Dyke), *Athena* (1954, MGM, Richard Thorpe), *Seven Brides for Seven Brothers* (1954, MGM, Stanley Donen), *West Side Story* (1961, United Artists, Robert Wise and Jerome Robbins), *Saturday Night Fever* (1977, Paramount, John Badham), *Grease* (1980, Paramount, Randall Kleiser), *Staying Alive* (1984, Paramount, Sylvester Stallone), *Dirty Dancing* (1987, Vestron, Emile Ardolino), *The Turning Point* (1977, Twentieth Century-Fox, Herbert Ross), *White Nights* (1987, Paramount, Taylor Hackford).

29. Films cited: *On the Town* (1950, MGM, Gene Kelly and Stanley Donen), *Take Me Out to the Ball Game* (1949, MGM, Busby Berkeley), *It's Always Fair Weather* (1955, MGM, Gene Kelly and Stanley Donen). For a more extended discussion of Gene Kelly and the "buddy" musical, see Steven Cohan's chapter, "Les Boys," in *Masked Men: American Masculinity and the Movies in the Fifties* (Indianapolis and Bloomington: Indiana University Press, forthcoming).

30. Films cited: *Singin' in the Rain* (1952, MGM, Gene Kelly and Stanley Donen), *An American in Paris* (1951, MGM, Vincente Minnelli), *Anchors Aweigh* (1945, MGM, George Sidney).

31. In *The Celluloid Closet: Homosexuality in the Movies*, rev. ed. (New York: Harper and Row, 1987), Vito Russo uncovers material on *Singin' in the Rain*'s production history that reveals that the erotics between Kelly and O'Connor were referred to in the original script: "One line of dialogue in Betty Comden and Adolph Green's screenplay for *Singin' in the Rain* (1952) was penciled out by the censors because it gave 'a hint of sexual perversion' between Donald O'Connor and Gene Kelly. When O'Connor gets the idea of dubbing the voice of Debbie Reynolds for the high-pitched, tinny voice of Jean Hagen in a proposed musical, *The Dancing Cavalier*, he illustrates his idea for Kelly by standing in front of Reynolds and mouthing the words to "Good Morning" while she sings behind him. When the song is over, O'Connor turns to Kelly and asks 'Well? Convincing?' Kelly, not yet catching on, takes it as a joke and replies, 'Enchanting! What are you doing later?' The joke was eliminated" (pp. 98–99).

32. Films cited: *That's Entertainment!* (1974, MGM, Jack Haley, Jr.), *Ziegfeld Follies* (1946, MGM, Vincente Minnelli), *That's Entertainment 2* (1976, MGM, Gene Kelly), *The Barkleys of Broadway* (1949, MGM, Charles Walters).

33. Film cited: *Calamity Jane* (1953, Warners, David Butler). Some lesbians also take what they would describe as a gay pleasure in musicals, and perform readings of individual films and of the genre in terms they identify as being influenced by their understanding of the ways gay men appreciate musicals. These kinds of gay approaches might take the form of specific star cult enthusiasms (for Judy Garland, Barbra Streisand, or Bette Midler, for example) that individual lesbian readers feel aren't important in lesbian culture, or of an appreciation for certain aesthetic or critical approaches (camp, for example) which seem unpopular, inoperative, or not "politically correct" in the lesbian culture(s) within which the individual reader places herself.

34. Lucie Arbuthnot and Gail Seneca, "Pre-text and Text in *Gentlemen Prefer Blondes*," *Film Reader* 5 (1982): 20. This essay is reprinted in *Issues in Feminist*

Film Criticism, ed. Patricia Erens (Bloomington and Indianapolis: Indiana University Press, 1990), 112–25.

35. Arbuthnot and Seneca, "Pre-text and Text," 21.

36. Ibid., 23.

37. Alix Stanton's "Blondes, Brunettes, Butches and Femmes" (unpublished seminar paper, Cornell University, 1991) offers a more extended consideration of butch-femme roles and cultures in relation to readings of *Gentlemen Prefer Blondes* (and *How to Marry a Millionaire* [1953, Twentieth Century-Fox, Jean Negulesco]).

38. Arbuthnot and Seneca, "Pre-text and Text," 21. For another approach to the lesbian aspects of this film, see Maureen Turim's "Gentlemen Consume Blondes," in *Issues in Feminist Film Criticism*, ed. Erens, 101–11; originally in *Wide Angle* 1, no. 1 (1979), also reprinted in *Movies and Methods, Volume II*, ed. Bill Nichols (Berkeley and Los Angeles: University of California Press, 1985): 369–78. As part of an addendum to the original article, Turim considers lesbianism and *Gentlemen Prefer Blondes* in light of certain feminist film theories about straight male spectatorship. Turim sees the main characters as male constructed "pseudo-lesbians," and the film's use of them as being related to "how lesbianism has served in male-oriented pornography to increase visual stimulation and to ultimately give twice as much power to the eye, which can penetrate even the liaisons which would appear to deny male entry" (pp. 110–11).

39. While not a lesbian-specific reading, Shari Roberts's "You Are My Lucky Star: Eleanor Powell's Brief Dance with Fame" (from an unpublished Ph.D. dissertation, "Seeing Stars: Female WWII Hollywood Musical Stars," University of Chicago, 1993) is suggestive of how and where such a reading might begin, with its discussion of Powell's (autoerotic) strength as a solo performer and its threatening qualities: "If . . . Powell represents a recognition of women as independent, working women, her films also reflect society's related fear of this 'new' woman, and potential gender confusion. . . . This anxiety is demonstrated with homophobic and cross-dressing jokes in the Powell films" (p. 7).

40. Films mentioned in this section: *The Gang's All Here* (1943, Twentieth Century-Fox, Busby Berkeley), *Dames* (1934, Warners, Ray Enright), *Fashions of 1934* (1934, Warners, William Dieterle), *42nd Street* (1933, Warners, Lloyd Bacon).

41. Feuer's "Gay Readings of Musicals" section in *Hollywood Musicals* (cited in note 27) concentrates on gay male production and reception of musicals.

42. Articles mentioned in this section: Richard Dyer, "Children of the Night: Vampirism as Homosexuality, Homosexuality as Vampirism," *Sweet Dreams: Sexuality, Gender and Popular Fiction*, ed. Susannah Radstone (London: Lawrence and Wishart, 1988), 47–72; Bonnie Zimmerman, "*Daughters of Darkness*: Lesbian Vampires," *Jump Cut* 24/25 (1981): 23–24; Sue-Ellen Case, "Tracking the Vampire," *differences* 3, no. 2 (Summer 1991): 1–20; Martin F. Norden, "Sexual References in James Whale's *Bride of Frankenstein*," *Eros in the Mind's Eye: Sexuality and the Fantastic in Art and Film*, ed. Donald Palumbo (New York: Greenwood Press, 1986), 141–50; Elizabeth Reba Weise, "Bisexuality, *The Rocky Horror Picture Show*, and Me," *Bi Any Other Name: Bisexual People Speak Out*, ed. Loraine Hutchins and Lani Kaahumanu (Boston: Alyson, 1991), 134–39.

43. Films mentioned in this section: *Vampyr* (1931, Gloria Film, Carl Theodore Dryer), *Dracula* (1931, Universal, Tod Browning), *Frankenstein* (1931, Universal, James Whale), *The Bride of Frankenstein* (1935, Universal, James Whale), *The Old*

Dark House (1932, Universal, James Whale), *The Invisible Man* (1933, Universal, James Whale). In light of the discussion of musicals in this essay, it is interesting to recall here that Whale's biggest success apart from his horror films was directing Universal's 1936 version of *Show Boat*.

44. Films and television series mentioned in this section: *Red River* (1948, United Artists, Howard Hawks), *Butch Cassidy and the Sundance Kid* (1969, Twentieth Century-Fox, George Roy Hill), *Laverne and Shirley* (1976–83, ABC), *Kate and Allie* (1984–90, CBS), *The Golden Girls* (1985–92, NBC).

2. Whose Text Is It Anyway?

1. Films cited: *The Women* (1939, MGM, George Cukor), *Craig's Wife* (1936, Columbia, Dorothy Arzner).

2. In his interview with Boze Hadleigh in *Conversations with My Elders* (New York: St. Martin's Press, 1986), Cukor asks what calling a homosexual "gay" means: "Does it mean a homosexual individual is frivolous, light-hearted, or has a good sense of humor?" (p. 138). Except where the material in this chapter refers directly to Cukor's sexual self-definition, however, I will use the term "gay" to refer to Cukor's homosexuality, although I still want to acknowledge the importance of being precise about historical and cultural differences in individual and group definitions of homosexuality, gayness, lesbianism, bisexuality, and queerness.

3. Implicitly in *Now You See It: Studies on Lesbian and Gay Film* (London and New York: Routledge, 1990), and explicitly in "Believing in Fairies: The Author and the Homosexual," in *Inside/Out: Lesbian Theories, Gay Theories*, ed. Diana Fuss (New York: Routledge, 1991), 185–201, Richard Dyer argues for the political and theoretical value of rethinking certain notions of authorship in discussing lesbian and gay filmmaking. While acknowledging the importance of individual and group readers in establishing queer cultural interpretive practices, Dyer's work is centered upon examining production practices and contexts. Of particular interest to Dyer is how and where notions of authorship (as a site of multiple authors "with varying degrees of hierarchy and control") and homosexuality (as "a culturally and historically specific phenomenon") might be applied to formulate a more precise sociocultural understanding of films made by and for lesbians and gays (p. 187).

4. For Barthes on the reader as "author" see (among other works): *S/Z*, trans. Richard Miller (New York: Hill and Wang, 1974); *Image-Music-Text*, ed. and trans. Stephen Heath (New York: Hill and Wang, 1977), particularly the "Death of the Author" and "From Work to Text" essays; and *The Pleasure of the Text*, trans. Richard Miller (New York: Hill and Wang, 1975).

5. Films cited: *Camille* (1937, MGM, George Cukor), *Little Women* (1933, RKO, George Cukor), *Christopher Strong* (1933, RKO, Dorothy Arzner), *Sylvia Scarlett* (1936, RKO, George Cukor), *Adam's Rib* (1949, MGM, George Cukor), *Dinner at Eight* (1933, MGM, George Cukor), *The Wild Party* (1929, Paramount, Dorothy Arzner), *A Star is Born* (1954, Warners, George Cukor), *A Woman's Face* (1941, MGM, George Cukor), *The Bride Wore Red* (1937, MGM, Dorothy Arzner), *Sarah and Son* (1930, Paramount, Dorothy Arzner).

6. The association of certain Hollywood stars with lesbian culture appears to be international. For example, a scene in the Japanese film *Early Summer* (1951, Shochiku, Yasujiro Ozu) has Noriko, the central character, being discussed by her

boss and her best friend. When the friend mentions that Noriko likes Katharine Hepburn, the boss matter-of-factly asks if Noriko is a lesbian.

7. Margie Adams, "Greta Garbo's 'Mysterious' Private Life," OUT/LOOK 4 (Fall 1990): 25. For another angle on lesbian star cults, see Victoria A. Brownworth's "Just Another Soapbox" column in the *PGN: Philadelphia Gay News* 16, no. 34 (June 19–25, 1992): 43. Brownworth uses the premiere of *Aliens 3* (1992, Twentieth Century-Fox, David Fincher) as a reason to discuss what she finds problematic about most dyke mass culture icons: "Now I know that this is treason amongst most lesbians who see Sigourney [Weaver] . . . and her 'Alien' character, Ripley, as leading lesbo ladies, but you girls need to get over these straight women and find some nice real-life lesbians to drool over. . . . The problem is this fixation lesbians have with pseudo-dykes, the great pretenders, the women who tell but don't kiss, the lesbo wanna-be's. . . . First we had this terrible attachment to Katharine Hepburn. Now that she's nearly dead we can adjust to the fact that she hates women other than herself and always has. She may have played a few cross-dressers, but she never was one in real life."

8. Of course, this is not to say some gays haven't made use of the knowledge of Arzner's lesbianism in conducting readings of her films, or that some lesbians haven't done the same with Cukor's "homosexuality" and his films. Here I am discussing more general trends in lesbian and gay cultural reading practices.

9. Two interesting works that examine lesbian cultures, lesbian reading practices, and mass culture (largely film) are Claire (formerly Judy) Whitaker's "Hollywood Transformed: Interviews with Lesbian Viewers," *Jump Cut* 24–25 (1981): 33–35; rpt. in *Jump Cut: Hollywood, Politics, and Counter-Cinema*, ed. Peter Stevens (New York: Praeger, 1981), 106–18; and Jane Cottis and Kaucyila Brooke's video *Dry Kisses Only* (1990). Whitaker's interviewees discuss their changing tastes and readings, and indicate how and where race and class intersect their readings of mass culture. Taken as a whole, these interviews suggest that stars and/or cross-gender identification are central to many lesbian uses of mass culture.

Dry Kisses Only combines mock-academic discussions, "lesbian on the street" interviews, and cleverly edited clips from films such as *The Great Lie* (1941, Warners, Edmund Goulding), *Johnny Guitar* (1954, Republic, Nicholas Ray), *All About Eve* (1950, Twentieth Century-Fox, Joseph L. Mankiewicz), *Mädchen in Uniform* (1931, Deutsche Film-Gemeinschaft, Leontine Sagan), and *The Hunger* (1983, MGM, Tony Scott) to reveal the variety and complexity of lesbian culture's confrontations with mass culture. Throughout the video, Cottis and Brooke suggest readings of films (including Arzner's *Christopher Strong*) that concentrate on lesbian culture and lesbian readers apart from any auteurist influences. Overall, the video implies that most lesbian cultural authorship in mass culture is conducted without reference to directors or even to stars, but rather is achieved by performing "perverse readings" articulating a text's "unconscious logic," "covert narrative," or "homosexual subplots or subtexts" through "searching out the look, the confrontation, the connotative language of the women onscreen," and looking for "disturbances" of the main (heterosexual) plot. However, these lesbian reading practices are very much like the interpretive practices of certain auteurist critics (discussed later in this section) who read films "obliquely," looking for "cracks" and "seams" in a text's "apparent formal coherence," which they would then attribute to a particular director's work on the project.

10. Judith Mayne, *The Woman at the Keyhole: Feminism and Women's Cinema* (Bloomington and Indianapolis: Indiana University Press, 1990), 89–123. An earlier version of this chapter appears as "Lesbian Looks: Dorothy Arzner and Female Authorship" in *How Do I Look? Queer Film and Video*, ed. Bad Object-Choices (Seattle: Bay Press, 1991), 103–35. A companion piece to these works is Mayne's "A Parallax View of Lesbian Authorship," in *Inside/Out: Lesbian Theories, Gay Theories*, ed. Diana Fuss (New York and London: Routledge, 1991), 173–84. This essay (re)considers authorship in relation to lesbian representation through discussions of "films in which the filmmaker herself is written into the text, although not in ways that match the common, easy equation between authorial presence and the fictions of identity" (p. 177).

11. Mayne, *Woman at the Keyhole*, 112–15.

12. Gerald Peary and Karyn Kay, "Interview with Dorothy Arzner," *The Work of Dorothy Arzner: Toward a Feminist Cinema*, ed. Claire Johnston (London: British Film Institute, 1975), 19–29.

13. Ibid., 26.

14. Cukor "outs" Arzner in his interview, telling Hadleigh that "our" Dorothy Arzner had an affair with Alla Nazimova (*Conversations*, 170). Other lengthy interviews with Cukor in books, and book-length studies of the director containing interview material, include Charles Higham and Joel Greenberg, *The Celluloid Muse: Hollywood Directors Speak* (New York: Signet/New American Library, 1969), 60–78; Andrew Sarris, *Interviews with Film Directors* (New York: Avon Books, 1967), 92–126; Gene D. Phillips, *George Cukor* (Boston: Twayne, 1982); Gary Carey, *Cukor & Co.: The Films of George Cukor and His Collaborators* (New York: Museum of Modern Art, 1971); Carlos Clarens, *George Cukor* (London: Secker and Warburg/British Film Institute, 1976); Gavin Lambert, *On Cukor* (New York: G. P. Putnam's Sons, 1972). Clarens also wrote "The Secret Life of George Cukor," containing interview material gathered by John Hofsess, for the gay porn magazine *Stallion* (August 1983). This article was perhaps the first evidence of Cukor's public coming out.

15. Patrick McGilligan, *George Cukor: A Double Life* (New York: St. Martin's Press, 1991).

16. Richard Lippe, "Cukor and Authorship: A Reappraisal," *CineAction!* 21–22 (Summer-Fall 1990): 26, 34.

17. Ibid., 24, 26.

18. Mayne, *Woman at the Keyhole*, 100.

19. Ibid., 102.

20. Jean-Luc Comolli and Jean Narboni, "Cinema/Ideology/Criticism," *Film Theory and Criticism*, 4th ed., ed. Gerald Mast, Marshall Cohen, and Leo Braudy (New York and Oxford: Oxford University Press, 1992), 687. This article originally appeared in English in Sylvia Harvey, ed., *May '68 and Film Culture* (London: British Film Institute, 1978).

21. Of course, discussing a director (or star) as a female or feminist auteur and/or as a lesbian, gay, bisexual, or queer auteur is to conduct auteurist analyses from within certain cultural, critical, and theoretical frames. But these practices would not necessarily be any more limited or limiting than other auteurist approaches that implicitly evaluated auteurs in relation to straight, white, male middle- and ruling-class ideological agendas, either to praise or to critique them. Feminist and queer auteurism foregrounds gender and sexualityas the terms of their analyses, and while these

analyses can become narrow and restrictive in their politics (for example, certain crit-ics deciding Gus Van Sant is not a good gay auteur because his films aren't "gay" or "gay-positive" enough), female-, feminist-, or queer-inflected auteurism can express as many different positions as there are women and queers.

One of the challenges for women and queers using auteurism is deciding what they mean by terms such as female, woman, or feminist auteur, or gay, lesbian, bisexual, or queer auteur. Will the directors (stars, writers, etc.) under auteurist consideration be evaluated against certain specific definitions of woman, the female, feminist, gay, lesbian, bisexual, or queer? Or, through a combination of textual analysis, biogra-phy, and cultural-historical contextualization, will auteurist critics suggest how they see auteurs defining these gender and sexual identity terms through their texts?

22. Films cited: *Dance, Girl, Dance* (1940, RKO, Dorothy Arzner), *Our Betters* (1933, RKO, George Cukor).

23. Mayne, *Woman at the Keyhole*, 112.

24. Ibid.

25. Ibid.

26. In *Dry Kisses Only*, Cottis and Brooke suggest a reading of *Christopher Strong* that concentrates on the work of lesbian culture and lesbian readers with no reference to auteurism. By excerpting clips from the film, Cottis and Brooke establish the re-lationship between Cynthia Darrington and Monica Strong as central to certain les-bian readings of the film.

27. Perhaps the best straight feminist reading of this film is Lucy Fischer's "*Dance, Girl, Dance*: When a Woman Looks," in *Shot/Countershot: Film Tradition and Women's Cinema* (Princeton: Princeton University Press, 1989), 148–54. Danny Peary also has a section on the film in *Cult Movies* (New York: Dell, 1981), 59–64, where he discusses its reputation as a feminist cult film.

28. Mayne, *Woman at the Keyhole*, 101.

29. On this point, Mayne finds that "Judy's attractions to men are shaped by sub-stitutions for women and female rivalry—Steve Adams is a professional mentor to substitute for Basilova, and Jimmie Harris is an infantile man who is desirable mainly because Bubbles wants him too" (*Woman at the Keyhole*, 103). My reading of these "substitutions" would note that Adams is coded as a feminized man whose trusted associate is the butch Miss Olmstead, and that it is less "female rivalry" than re-pressed queer desire on Bubbles's part that makes *her* find Jimmie "desirable mainly because" she notices Judy's interest in him. Besides, Judy's wish on a star after a date with Jimmie is for a dancing career, not for him. As for Basilova, it is worth noting in this context that her removal from the plot is accomplished in classic ho-mophobic narrative fashion: she gets hit by an oncoming bus as she takes Judy to her ballet audition. As if to comment on Basilova's (un)expected death, Arzner moves from her body to pan up the phallic building across the street that houses the ballet company.

30. Mayne's reading of this moment is feminist, but not lesbian: "And the catfight that erupts between Judy and Bubbles on stage is less a recuperative move . . . than the claiming by two women of the stage as an extension of their conflicted friendship, rather than as the alienated site of performance" (*Woman at the Keyhole*, 102). Al-though concerned with examining the "lesbian inflection" in Arzner's treatment of "female bonding" as part of how the director expresses the tensions between female

friendships and lesbianism, Mayne discusses Bubbles's and Judy's bond as an example of heterosexual female rivalry.

31. Sarah Halprin, in "Writing in the Margins," *Jump Cut* 29 (1984), notes that there are "two 'minor' characters [in *Dance, Girl, Dance*] who both dress and look remarkably similar to Arzner herself (i.e., tailored, 'mannish,' in the manner of Radclyffe Hall and other famous lesbians of the time), and are placed as mature, single, independent women who are crucial to the career of the young Judy and who are clearly seen as oppressed by social stereotyping, of which they are contemptuous" (p. 32). Basilova is one of these butch women, and Miss Olmstead is the other. It is Olmie who first jumps up to applaud Judy's tirade against the burlesque house audience.

32. Film cited: *Salome* (1922, Nazimova Productions, Charles Bryant).

33. Peary and Kay, "Interview," 25.

34. Is it just a coincidence that the 1921 film version of *Camille* starred another lesbian-bisexual team, Alla Nazimova and Rudolph Valentino, as Marguerite and Armand? Cukor's response to Hadleigh's question "Why is Armand so often played by gay actors?" is: "Not just actors—Nureyev opposite Margot Fonteyn . . . I don't know. Perhaps because it's so romantic a part, and the character has a sensitivity that some actors can't put across" (*Conversations*, 135).

35. Lambert, *On Cukor*, 109–10.

36. Films cited: *Queen Christina* (1933, MGM, Rouben Mamoulian), *Love* (1927, MGM, Edmund Goulding), *Anna Karenina* (1935, MGM, Clarence Brown). In "Garbo and Phallic Motherhood: A 'Homosexual' Visual Economy," *Screen* 29, no. 3 (Summer 1988): 14–39, Peter Matthews discusses Garbo's star image and its appeal to gay men in terms of both Freudian and feminist psychoanalytic theories: "If, in the most obvious way, Garbo-identification licenses the male gay audience to 'possess' all her gorgeous young men (John Gilbert, Robert Taylor, *et al.*) as fetish objects, that by no means exhausts her power as an object of wish-fulfillment. For both women and gay men, she can also be the inspirer of 'Oedipal nostalgia.' Andrew Britton has situated the Garbo persona in the literary and theatrical legend of *la divine*—that sublimely androgynous 'male muse' who helps the male poet to recover his pre-Oedipal polymorphous sexuality in an 'ecstatic renunciation of gender.' . . . But if *la divine* seems in this sense to be a *gay* muse renewing the precocious seductions of the Mother, offering herself simultaneously as the subject and object of a 'perverse' pre-Oedipal fantasy, the specific regression that she enables is in fact potentially available to everyone in her audience" (p. 26). With this last sentence, as well as with the notion of "renunciation of gender," Matthews suggests that his gay readings of Garbo are open to broader queer applications, as Garbo's narrativized image can potentially trigger "perverse" fantasies in *any* susceptible viewer.

37. Carey, *Cukor & Co.*, 65.

38. In his essay "The Lady of the Camellias" (*A Barthes Reader*, ed. Susan Sontag [New York: Hill and Wang, 1982]), Roland Barthes makes a passing connection between Marguerite and gays that suggests one possible source for understanding the type of gay identification with Marguerite I discuss here: "Marguerite lives in the awareness of her alienation, she lives only through it: she knows herself to be, and in a sense *wills* herself to be a courtesan. And the behavior she adopts in order to adjust consists entirely in behavior meant to secure recognition: now she endorses her own

legend exaggeratedly, and plunges into the whirlwind of the typical courtesan's life (like those homosexuals whose way of accepting their condition is to make it obvious)" (p. 91).

39. The following comment by Carlos Clarens reveals a rhetorical sleight of hand typical of criticism about Cukor and his films in which gayness (of the director, of a character, of an actor) is simultaneously invoked and rendered invisible: "Rex O'Malley plays Gaston, Marguerite's devoted dandy, with that familiar tact and delicacy that stamps him right away as the Cukor Other Man, sympathetic and sexless" (*George Cukor*, 50).

40. Hadleigh, *Conversations*, 164.

41. Reviews as quoted in Peary, *Cult Movies*, 331.

42. Ibid., 333.

43. Ibid.

44. Ibid.

45. Ibid.

46. Carey, *Cukor & Co.*, 53.

47. Clarens, *George Cukor*, 143.

48. Lambert, *On Cukor*, 92.

49. Ibid.

50. Films cited: *A Bill of Divorcement* (1932, RKO, George Cukor), *Pat and Mike* (1952, MGM, George Cukor). A related reflection on film history occurs to me here: frequently queer-positioned director Lowell Sherman (*The Greeks Had a Word for Them*, 1932, RKO; Mae West's *She Done Him Wrong*, 1933, Paramount) worked with Hepburn on *Morning Glory*, the film that officially won her the 1932–33 Best Actress Oscar. The finale of *Morning Glory* had Hepburn's character, Eva Lovelace, renouncing the men interested in her so she can devote herself to an acting career. Eva Lovelace is an interesting name, suggestive of woman in her Christian originary state erotically connected to something traditionally feminine. Perhaps Hepburn as Eva is the femme side of Jo March and Cynthia Darrington.

The Oscar voters in 1933 were clearly more comfortable publicly rewarding Hepburn's portrayal of what could be read as a more traditionally feminine character, although just as clearly they were silently casting their ballots for Hepburn's compelling butchness in *Little Women* and *Christopher Strong*, which were released during the same Oscar-qualifying period as *Morning Glory*. Another queer culture Oscar footnote is in order here: the Best Actor winner the same year that butch, man-renouncing Hepburn was named Best Actress was gay actor Charles Laughton, for his near-parodic, tongue-in-cheek portrayal of that notorious, hypermacho, much-married monarch, Henry VIII.

What was happening in the West, and in Western cultural production, in the early 1930s that encouraged such queer goings-on? Are there links to the Depression, with its disruptive challenges to capitalist patriarchal hegemony? Or does it have something to do with the effects of the more liberal pre-1934 Production Code in Hollywood? Or might this situation be the result of a growing sense of community within the film industry on both sides of the Atlantic among prominent queers and queer-positive straights, such as David O. Selznick, producer of certain Arzner and Cukor films? Questions such as these might be researched and explored at greater length as part of authoring a queer history of film and other forms of mass culture.

3. *I Love* Laverne and Shirley

1. Vivian Vance, "Lucy and I Adored Each Other—Then People Began to Whisper That We Were Lovers," *National Enquirer* (August 29, 1989): 20. There is background commentary in this article by an anonymous *Enquirer* staff writer that Vance clearly did not write.

2. Ibid.

3. Ibid., 20–21.

4. One of the more recent uses of Lucy and Ethel that capitalizes upon their lesbian aura (as well as their gay cult status) is an ad for AIDS Project Los Angeles, which features a still of the pair looking at each other as they struggle to carry a large fish (from the "Deep-Sea Fishing" episode, November 19, 1956). The main caption, "Be A Buddy And Help Someone Out," is followed by copy beginning: "What makes life so much better is sharing it with a Buddy. Laughing. Crying. Talking. Holding. Going to dinner. Taking in a movie. Having fun." This public service ad has been featured in issues of the gay magazine *Genre* (the April/May 1991 issue, for example), as well as in other gay and lesbian publications.

5. Robert H. Deming, "*Kate and Allie*: 'New Women' and the Audience's Television Archive," *Camera Obscura* 16 (January 1988): 157.

6. Representative of the publicity accorded Burke's "feud" with *Designing Women*'s cast and crew, and her subsequent firing, is *People* magazine's coverage by Elizabeth Sporkin, Lois Armstrong, Tom Cunnett, and Jack Kelly (36, no. 3 [July 29, 1991]: 46–51), which uses "Why They Dumped Delta" as the front-page headline for its "Odd Woman Out" story—a title evoking that of Ann Bannon's famous lesbian novel *Odd Girl Out*.

7. Quoted in Charles Higham and Joel Greenberg, *The Celluloid Muse: Hollywood Directors Speak* (New York: Signet/New American Library, 1972), 63.

8. The following is a partial list of American situation comedies I would consider lesbian sitcoms:

The Girls, 1950, CBS; *I Love Lucy*, 1951–57, CBS; *My Friend Irma*, 1952–54, CBS; *It's Always Jan*, 1955–56, CBS; *Those Whiting Girls*, 1955–57, CBS; *The Gale Storm Show*, 1956–60, CBS/ABC; *How To Marry a Millionaire*, 1957–59, syndicated; *My Sister Eileen*, 1960–61, CBS; *The Lucy Show*, 1962–68, CBS; *The Patty Duke Show*, 1963–66, ABC; *Petticoat Junction*, 1963–70, CBS; *Bewitched*, 1964–72, ABC; *The Flying Nun*, 1967–70, ABC; *The Mothers-in-Law*, 1967–69, NBC; *Here's Lucy*, 1968–74, CBS; *The Mary Tyler Moore Show*, 1970–77, CBS; *Rhoda*, 1974–78, CBS; *Phyllis*, 1975–77, CBS; *Alice*, 1976–85, CBS; *Laverne and Shirley*, 1976–83, ABC; *The Betty White Show*, 1977–78, CBS; *Sugar Time!*, 1977–78, ABC; *The Roller Girls*, 1978, NBC; *Goodtime Girls*, 1980, ABC; *It's a Living*, 1980–82, ABC and syndicated; *Private Benjamin*, 1981–83, CBS; *Square Pegs*, 1982–83, CBS; *Kate and Allie*, 1984–90, CBS; *The Golden Girls*, 1985–92, NBC; *227*, 1986–89, NBC; *Designing Women*, 1986–present, CBS; *Roseanne*, 1988–present, ABC; *Sugar 'n' Spice*, 1990, NBC; *Babes*, 1990–91, Fox; *Princesses*, 1991, CBS; *Sibs*, 1991–92, ABC; *Good and Evil*, 1991, ABC; *Nurses*, 1991–present, NBC; *Room for Two*, 1992–present, ABC; *Golden Palace*, 1992-present, CBS.

9. Adrienne Rich, "Compulsory Heterosexuality and Lesbian Existence," *Powers of Desire: The Politics of Sexuality*, ed. Ann Sitnow, Christine Stansell, and Sharon Thompson (New York: Monthly Review Press, 1983), 192. To a certain extent, queer rhetorical-political strategies have led me to adopt and adapt Rich's les-

bian continuum in this section, particularly because it rejects the idea that what is called "homosocial" is really fully distinct from what is called "homosexual." At present, straight culture's careful maintenance of the line between homosociality and homosexuality only encourages homophobia and heterocentrism, as the homosocial is always considered preferable to the homosexual. If there wasn't some problem about being labeled "homosexual," straight culture wouldn't care if certain straight personal relationships and cultural representations were misperceived as being queer. As this clearly is not the case until there are pervasive signs that queer labels have ceased to be hysteria-inducing to straights, any same-sex intensities in life or in cultural representation I will call "homosexual," "lesbian," "gay," "bisexual," or "queer." Lesbian and gay maintenance of the homosexual/heterosexual line is another matter, as this is concerned with keeping same-sex sex as the central definer of queerness in order to prevent the cultural and political neutralization and domestication of lesbianism and gayness by straight culture.

10. Ibid.

11. Another aspect of specifically lesbian cultural spectatorship practices I will not directly address here is readings of characters and shows developed around erotic attraction and desire. Gail Sausser, in the "Movie and T.V. Heart-Throbs" section of *Lesbian Etiquette* (Trumansburg, N.Y.: Crossing Press, 1986), includes some brief comments that highlight these types of lesbian pleasures in television situation comedies: "I also had a crush on Morticia Addams (Carolyn Jones) of *The Addams Family*. You've got to love a woman who has pet man-eating plants and only lets her husband kiss her hand. . . . Do you remember *The Patty Duke Show?* Patty's charms never overwhelmed me, but I do know certain lesbians who were in love with her. I loved Elizabeth Montgomery on *Bewitched*, but like her mother, Endora, I never could understand what she saw in 'Derwood.' Barbara Eden on *I Dream of Jeannie* was another crush of mine, no matter how politically incorrect her role was. It's amazing to think of the latter two women's roles: both had incredible magical powers, but chose to be subservient to bumbling men who ordered them around. And speaking of politically incorrect, I won't mention the name of the person who had a crush on Tina Louise a.k.a. 'Ginger' on *Gilligan's Island*, but I do see it as a forerunner to her current crush on Joan Collins" (p. 59). It is clear from Sausser's list that lesbian erotic pleasures in situation comedies are not necessarily focused on those programs I am calling "lesbian sitcoms," whose women-centered narrative construction encourages other types of queer audience positioning and pleasure in nonlesbian audiences.

12. Marilyn R. Farwell, "Heterosexual Plots and Lesbian Subtexts: Toward a Theory of Lesbian Narrative Space," *Lesbian Texts and Contexts: Radical Revisions*, ed. Karla Jay and Joanne Glasgow (New York and London: New York University Press, 1990), 95.

13. Mimi White, "Ideological Analysis and Television," *Channels of Discourse*, ed. Robert Allen (Chapel Hill: University of North Carolina Press, 1987), 162.

14. Not mentioned in this section are those gay readings of many of these sitcoms which interpret the women characters as gay men. Developed within cultural contexts that foster (imposed or chosen) cross-gender identification, these "women-as-gay-men" readings of mass culture have been, and still are, common in gay culture. See note 13 to chapter five ("The Sissy Boy, the Fat Ladies, and the Dykes") for a longer discussion of these reading practices.

15. Christine Holmlund, "When Is a Lesbian Not a Lesbian?: The Lesbian Continuum and the Mainstream Femme Film," *Camera Obscura* 25/26 (January-May 1991): 145–46.

16. Danae Clark, "Commodity Lesbianism," *Camera Obscura* 25/26 (January-May 1991): 192.

17. Promotional advertisement. *TV Guide* (Central Pennsylvania edition) 40, no. 15 (April 11–17, 1992): 148–49.

18. I borrow the term "hypothetical lesbian" from Chris Straayer's "*Voyage en Douce, Entre Nous*: The Hypothetical Lesbian Heroine," *Jump Cut* 35 (1990): 50.

19. Between *I Love Lucy* and *The Lucy Show*, *The Lucy-Desi Comedy Hour* ran for three seasons (1957–60) and thirteen episodes. These shows most often relegated Ethel (and Fred) to the sidelines, while featuring guest stars, often celebrity couples: Ida Lupino/Howard Duff, June Haver/Fred MacMurray, Betty Grable/Harry James. While their narratives were more straight-couple oriented, these programs occasionally recalled *I Love Lucy*'s Lucy-Ethel lesbian narrative and performative dynamics, as when Lucy forms temporary alliances with her women guest stars in order to get around their husbands. In the "Lucy Wins a Racehorse" episode (February 3, 1958), for example, Betty Grable lends Lucy the money she needs to care for a horse Little Ricky wants, but which "Big" Ricky wants to get rid of. "Betty, you're just what I've been looking for," a grateful Lucy exclaims, "an Ethel Mertz with money!"

20. During the run of *The Lucy Show*, Viv and/or Lucy were involved in many activities that could be read in specifically lesbian cultural terms: playing softball, coaching sports teams, doing home repair work, volunteer firefighting, playing competitive pool, and being WAVEs in World War II. Viv also played Antony to Lucy's Cleopatra in an all-woman, volunteer firefighter production of Shakespeare's *Antony and Cleopatra*. A 1992 promotional ad for reruns of *The Lucy Show* on the Nickelodeon cable channel had an announcer intoning "Lucy . . . Vivian . . . Two single women, living on the edge—together" over a shot of Vivian tumbling on top of Lucy. It makes a person wonder if the "double pink triangle" diamond Nickelodeon used as part of its "Nick at Night" logo during this ad was just a coincidence.

21. Patricia Mellencamp, "Situation Comedy, Feminism, and Freud: Discourses of Gracie and Lucy," *Studies in Entertainment*, ed. Tania Modleski (Bloomington and Indianapolis: Indiana University Press, 1986), 90. Ball often remarked that her favorite impersonation was of Tallulah Bankhead. She even hired Bankhead for an episode of *The Lucy-Desi Comedy Hour* titled "The Celebrity Next Door" (December 3, 1957). This identification with Bankhead through imitating her voice is interesting as it suggests something of what is covered up in the narratives and major women characters of *I Love Lucy*, *The Lucy Show*, and *Here's Lucy*.

In her discussion of the narrativization of the female voice in films as a process that carefully contains that voice by synchronizing it with and suturing it to the body, Kaja Silverman mentions certain transgressions from this patriarchal auditory regime: "This vocal corporalization is to be distinguished from that which gives the sounds emitted by Mae West, Marlene Dietrich, or Lauren Bacall their distinctive quality, since in each of these last instances it is a 'male' rather than 'female' body which is deposited in the voice. Otherwise stated, the lowness and huskiness of each of these three voices connote masculinity rather than femininity, so that the voice seems to exceed the gender of the body from which it proceeds. That excess confers upon it a privileged status vis-à-vis both language and sexuality" (*The Acoustic Mir-*

ror [Bloomington and Indianapolis: Indiana University Press, 1988], 61). Of course, Tallulah Bankhead could be added to this list of vocally "masculine" transgressors. Her well-documented private life was also marked by "excess," much of it relating to her bisexuality and her affinity for queers and queer cultures. Ball's penchant for imitating Bankhead finds outlets on her series, as in one episode of *I Love Lucy*, "Lucy Fakes Illness" (January 28, 1952), where Bankhead's is one personality that emerges when Lucy pretends to have amnesia (another is Katharine Hepburn). Pretense or not, however, the Bankhead model, with its subversive implications for gender and sexuality, is revealed as being inside Lucy.

22. This narrative pattern of marginalizing men and emphasizing women-bonding in these situation comedies' maternity and birth episodes reflects existing Western cultural practices which, until recently, have confined men (apart from doctors and their assistants) to the "waiting room." *I Love Lucy* acknowledges this male marginalization and alienation, with its attendant woman-envy, in the "Ricky Has Labor Pains" episode (May 1, 1953). During Lucy's sixth month, Ricky develops periods of nausea, dizzy spells, and stomach cramps. A doctor tells Lucy that Ricky's symptoms are psychosomatic, and suggests she make him the "center of attention" for a while. So Lucy arranges a "daddy shower" with the help of Ethel's husband, Fred. But, disguised as male reporters, Lucy and Ethel invade the all-male space of the "daddy shower," reminding us that in lesbian sitcom narratives, men can become the "center of attention" only temporarily.

23. Adrienne Rich has some provocative thoughts about maternal erotics: "If women are the earliest sources of emotional caring and physical nurture for both female and male children, it would seem logical, from a feminist perspective at least, to pose the following questions: whether the search for love and tenderness in both sexes does not originally lead toward women; *why in fact women would ever redirect that search*. . . . I doubt that enough feminist scholars and theorists have taken the pains to acknowledge the societal forces that wrench women's emotional and erotic energies away from themselves and other women and from women-identified values" (p. 183). Implicit in Rich's words here is the question of why more, if not all, women aren't lesbian. The comedies I am treating here create situations in which the women all are, in a manner of speaking, lesbian, if not "actually," then in the way their relationships develop, and are developed by, narratives that position audiences to take queer pleasures in the series.

24. Serafina Bathrick's "*The Mary Tyler Moore Show*: Women at Home and at Work," *MTM: 'Quality Television'*, ed. Jane Feuer, Paul Kerr, and Tise Vahimagi (London: British Film Institute, 1984), 99–131, provides an excellent straight feminist analysis of the series. While Bathrick sees Mary as a character who moves between an all-woman "family" at home and a male-dominated patriarchal "family" at work, she consistently emphasizes "the ways in which Mary's female friendships are privileged in this series," with Phyllis and Rhoda providing "particularly significant alternatives to romantic or marital relations" (p. 118).

25. One male character on *The Mary Tyler Moore Show* who is referred to constantly, but whom the audience never sees, is Phyllis's husband, Dr. Lars Lindstrom. This narrative decision makes Mary's home life totally women-centered, with dates and male coworkers becoming only temporary visitors.

26. Richard Corliss, "Happy Days Are Here Again," *Television: The Critical View*, ed. Horace Newcomb (New York: Oxford University Press, 1982), 70.

27. The narrative use of gays and gayness as markers of another queer agenda is common in lesbian sitcoms. Perhaps this reflects the ways in which lesbianism has been more persistently rendered invisible in straight culture than gayness has been. As a result, mass culture texts often have gays and gayness stand in for all queer identities and all forms of queerness. From *The Mary Tyler Moore Show* onward, it is a rare lesbian sitcom that doesn't invoke or represent gayness regularly, while repressing any unmistakable codes of lesbianism entirely, relegating lesbianism to suggestive jokes, or containing it in those special "lesbian episodes" referred to earlier in this section. Perhaps more frequent lesbian innuendo or more overt lesbian representation on these shows would threaten many viewers by making manifest the queerness of their pleasures in these shows.

As for specific examples of gayness also representing a show's more fundamental lesbian queerness, besides those connotative readings of Ted and Murray as gay, *The Mary Tyler Moore Show* plays with gay innuendo in the "Menage-à-Phyllis" episode (discussed in this chapter), and provides Phyllis with a gay brother who becomes fast friends with Rhoda, which is perhaps the program's acknowledgment of Rhoda's status as a cult figure for the show's gay audience. *Laverne and Shirley* has gay characters appear in various episodes—the actor in the army training film, a snooty boutique salesman to whom Shirley says, "We girls wouldn't want to buy something from a man who smells like the inside of my grandmother's purse." Many viewers also read upstairs neighbors Lenny and Squiggy as a gay pair. *The Golden Girls* has a gay houseboy on its pilot episode, and Blanche's gay brother appears on two shows, once with his future male spouse. Anthony Bouvier, the one regular male character on *Designing Women*, besides being black, is also heavily gay-coded, with most of the innuendo centering on his time in prison.

During its 1990–91 season, *Roseanne* gives the title character a gay boss in a long-term relationship (the character was dropped after the 1991–92 season). Predictably enough, in terms of lesbian sitcom narrative repression and substitution, these men are introduced on an episode that takes great pains to heterosexualize Roseanne's tomboy-butch, baseball-playing daughter Darlene by having her tell her mother that she likes boys, but she refuses to go to a formal dance because all the fuss involved in dressing feminine makes her feel strange. Roseanne's police officer (and, later, truck driver) sister, Jackie, had already undergone some heterosexualizing in the previous season, but Roseanne's comment to Darlene in response to her decision not to go to the dance reminds us of what is being repressed: "I think you've been hanging out with Aunt Jackie too much!"

Intertexual events have been at work since the series' premiere that both reveal and support the lesbian charge of *Roseanne*. For example, Laurie Metcalf, who plays Jackie, was cast as a (sympathetic) lesbian police officer in *Internal Affairs* (1990, Paramount, Mike Figgis), a film that also has a gay erotic text. Then there are two pieces that appeared in issues of *Parade* magazine (a Sunday supplement in many local American newspapers). In the September 15, 1991, section "Personality Parade," a reader asks columnist Walter Scott, "With all the concern about AIDS, I was surprised when two gay characters turned up on the 'Roseanne' show. My husband says this proves what he's always suspected—that Roseanne is gay. I don't believe it. Who's right?" Scott's answer, in part, is: "You are. Roseanne Barr Arnold's real-life brother and sister are homosexuals, however, and she says, 'My show seeks to portray various slices of life, and homosexuals are a reality' " (p. 2). Lynn Minton's January

26, 1992, "What We Care About," a feature column in "Fresh Voices" devoted to teenagers' questions and viewpoints, asks Sara Gilbert, who plays Darlene, "Are you a tomboy?" While Gilbert answers "no," she admits "most of my friends are guys . . . with them I feel comfortable. If one of them shows up, I can, like, roll out of bed and not have to take a shower" (p. 4). This sounds just like something Darlene would say—and reflects the character's general attitude toward boys on the show, which is friendly but not romantic. Later in 1992, Gilbert was featured in the film *Poison Ivy* (New Line, Kati Shea Ruben), which places her character in a lesbian-suggestive relationship with Drew Barrymore.

28. Vince Waldron, *Classic Sitcoms* (New York: Macmillan, 1987), 151.

29. *Mary Tyler Moore* spinoffs *Rhoda, Phyllis,* and *The Betty White Show* each developed lesbian narratives. *Rhoda* is particularly interesting because the first show simultaneously establishes the series's potential narrative center as the relationship between Rhoda, her sister Brenda (whom she lives with), and their mother, while it also introduces a steady romantic interest for Rhoda in the form of Joe Gerard, the owner of a wrecking company. Joe and Rhoda marry in the first season, and episodes in the next two seasons reflect the tensions between the demands of lesbian narrative construction and the requirements of a heterosexual-couple sitcom. After a short, frustrating period as a housewife, Rhoda begins her own window-dressing business with an old school friend, Myrna Morgenstein. And she still maintains close ties with her sister (they live in the same building) and with her mother.

However, it soon became apparent to the show's creators that Rhoda (and actress Valerie Harper) wasn't the only one frustrated with the character's married life. CBS president Fred Silverman felt that the idea of Rhoda marrying was "the worst programming idea ever . . . the moment she fell in love and got married the whole series lost its bite. The source of all the comedic conflict on the show was gone. The stunt hurt the show" (quoted in Feuer, Kerr, and Vahimagi, *MTM*, 209). While the show was initially popular with audiences, second thoughts among *Rhoda*'s producers and writers convinced them to gradually move the show back to its (lesbian) roots. Joe and Rhoda separate, then divorce. During Joe and Rhoda's estrangement, airline stewardess Sally Gallagher is introduced as Rhoda's new friend. But *Rhoda*'s last two seasons reveal a series only uncertainly committed to developing its lesbian narrative space, as Las Vegas entertainer Johnny Venture becomes Rhoda's sometime boyfriend, Sally and Brenda begin going out on regular dates with Gary Levy, and Brenda develops a steady relationship with an accordion player.

30. Waldron, *Classic Sitcoms*, 141, 147, 153, 159, 166, 173.

31. For anyone interested in exploring butch and femme cultures, styles, and attitudes, a good place to start is *The Persistent Desire: A Butch-Femme Reader,* ed. Joan Nestle (Boston: Alyson, 1992). In addition, three valuable articles are Joan Nestle's "The Fem Question," *Pleasures and Dangers: Exploring Female Sexuality,* ed. Carole Vance (London: Pandora Press, 1989), 232–41; Sue-Ellen Case's "Toward a Butch-Femme Aesthetic," *Discourse* 11, no. 1 (Fall-Winter 1988–89): 55–71; and Madeline Davis and Elizabeth Lapovsky Kennedy's "Oral History and the Study of Sexuality in the Lesbian Community: Buffalo, New York, 1940–1960," *Hidden from History: Reclaiming the Lesbian and Gay Past,* ed. Martin Bauml Duberman, Martha Vicinus, and George Chauncey, Jr. (New York: New American Library, 1989), 426–40. Joan Nestle's autobiographical *A Restricted Country* (Ithaca, N.Y.: Firebrand

Books, 1987) also contains a wealth of observations and insights regarding butch and femme identities and relationships.

A production history note by Richard Corliss in "Happy Days" suggests that a heterosexualized version of butch-femme dynamics may have been in the minds of *Laverne and Shirley* cocreators Garry Marshall and Mark Rothman as they devised Cindy Williams's Shirley Feeney as a character "who could express both slapstick and sentiment, who was both Lucille Ball and Mary Tyler Moore. The idea here was to put a Mary Richards character into Lucy situations, and to play her adorable fastidiousness against a more pragmatic good-time-Charlotte colleague: Penny Marshall's Laverne DeFazio" (p. 72). This quote also makes it clear that Marshall and Rothman understood the sitcom lineage of their show and its characters.

32. A similar moment occurs at the end of *Gentlemen Prefer Blondes* (1953, Twentieth Century-Fox, Howard Hawks) when after a double wedding, the camera tracks in from a shot of the two male-female couples to frame a tight two shot of best friends Lorelei Lee (Marilyn Monroe) and Dorothy Shaw (Jane Russell) exchanging tender looks as the film fades to black. For a good lesbian-feminist reading of this film see Lucy Arbuthnot and Gail Seneca's "Pre-text and Text in *Gentlemen Prefer Blondes*," *Film Reader* 5 (1982): 13–23; rpt. in *Issues in Feminist Film Criticism*, ed. Patricia Erens (Bloomington and Indianapolis: Indiana University Press, 1990), 112–25.

33. Marriage is usually a threat to the narrative pleasures of lesbian sitcoms. This holds true even if the major women characters are already married when the series debuts. The comic high points on *I Love Lucy* occur when Ethel and Lucy ignore, resist, or temporarily escape the demands of being wives. On lesbian sitcoms featuring unmarried women, the marriage of one of them often signals that a series will end in a season or two, as was the case with *Laverne and Shirley*, *Kate and Allie*, and even *Rhoda*, in a way. Perhaps learning from its predecessors, *The Golden Girls* ended its seven-year run with Dorothy's wedding, about which Bea Arthur (who plays Dorothy) commented, "That's the way they're going to get rid of me — which is better, I guess, than having me killed off in a flaming car wreck or something" (*Entertainment Tonight*, April 15, 1992, ABC).

Even talk of an engagement on these sitcoms becomes a narrative crisis for the women characters and a source of anxiety for viewers, who consciously or not realize an engagement or a marriage would change these women's relationships to each other, and therefore their own relationship to the show — and not for the better. When it comes down to it, any sort of romantic or sexual situation with a man on these programs, including dating, is disruptive. Appearances by ex-husbands are different because they usually strengthen the bonds between women by reinforcing the undesirability of heterosexual unions, as *Kate and Allie*, *The Golden Girls*, and *Designing Women* have shown.

34. Since Laverne's "company" on the last years of the show is almost exclusively male, the series develops an interesting gay text, with the characters Lenny and Squiggy (already read as a gay pair by some viewers), Carmine, and Mr. De Fazio taking up more and more narrative space. A number of episodes feature these male characters while marginalizing Laverne, or positioning her as "one of the boys" butchly performing comic stunt work and rough physical comedy. There are a few episodes during the final seasons that attempt to recreate the butch-femme dynamics of Laverne and Shirley by substituting Rhonda, the blonde starlet-next-door, for Shir-

ley. One episode has Laverne possessed by the spirit of a man during a seance. While in this cross-gender mental state, Laverne kisses Rhonda.

35. The term "compulsory heterosexuality" is from Adrienne Rich's essay "Compulsory Heterosexuality and Lesbian Existence," *Signs* 5, no. 4 (Summer 1980); rpt. in Snitow, Stansell, and Thompson, *Powers of Desire*, 177–205.

36. For typical popular press coverage of the Burke-*Designing Women* situation see articles such as "Odd Woman Out," *People* (cited in this chapter's note 6); Mary Murphy and Frank Swertlow, "Delta Redesigned," *TV Guide* 40, no. 27 (July 4–10, 1992): 10–16; Susan Littwin, "Not Just Whistlin' Dixie," *TV Guide* 38, no. 50 (December 15, 1990): 4–5, 7, 9–10; Elaine Warren, "Shake-Up At the Sugarbakers: It's Now Re-*Designing Women*," *TV Guide* 39, no. 38 (September 21, 1991): 10–17.

37. This reference to Lucy and Ethel is only one of a number of allusions in *Designing Women* to the series's lesbian sitcom predecessors. For example, the end of one episode finds Mary Jo, Charlene, and Julia deciding to protect Suzanne from possible arrest by saying they were with her when a fire broke out at the Design House exhibit. When Mary Jo says they are like the Four Musketeers, "all for one and one for all," everyone emotionally embraces each other in a big circle. "Isn't this sweet," Charlene comments from within the circle, "I feel like we're on the last episode of *The Mary Tyler Moore Show.*"

Another episode begins with Charlene ordering videos from the *I Love Lucy* fan club. "I love Lucy!" Charlene exclaims. Julia replies, "I love Ethel, too," after which she admits she wouldn't mind watching the videotapes with Charlene when they arrive. Later in the same episode, the cast wonders how they can stop an unscrupulous photographer from printing some racy pictures for which he's flattered them into posing. Charlene comments that if the photographer had taken "pictures of Lucy and Ethel, they'd find a way to get the film back." This remark inspires the photographer's assistant, Estelle, to help the women: "Of course, Lucy and Ethel would steal the film!" Deciding to substitute her own photographs of "The Women of Atlanta" (the episode's title) for those of the male photographer, Estelle tells Mary Jo, Charlene, Julia, and Suzanne she didn't know she liked Southern women, and that they "should get together more often." The episode ends with Estelle's pictures shown in a montage, followed by a still of Lucy dressed as a hillbilly, which acts both as an homage to Lucy and as a reference to Charlene, who is from the mountains of Missouri.

38. "Julia Duffy Leaving 'Designing Women,' " *New York Daily News*, rpt. in *The Morning Call* (Allentown, Pa.), March 27, 1992, D2.

39. Even after Duffy's departure, however, *Designing Women*'s (pseudo?) dyke saga continued. In its seventh season opener (September 25, 1992), the series introduced new regular Judith Ivey as B. J. Poteet, a rich widow who hires the Sugarbaker firm to redecorate her mansion. A late-night business meeting at B. J.'s home quickly turns into a drunken party, with Julia playing cards and smoking cigars, Mary Jo sitting on Julia's lap, and the whole cast partying in the mansion's hidden sexual bondage room.

4. The Gay Straight Man

1. *An Early Frost* (1985, ABC, John Erman). The line quoted here gains added resonance, as it is delivered by Sylvia Sidney, a gay cult(ure) figure.

2. Benny himself may have been queer. In an interview with Boze Hadleigh, comic actor Paul Lynde recalls a note he received from Benny after one of his *Carol*

Burnett Show appearances: "It was so complimentary, so lovely . . . but ya know, we could never have worked together. It wouldn't work—too lavender, with two old queens together." Lynde goes on to comment on the Mary Livingstone biography of Benny: "Yes, the truth about *that* will be a long time coming. I mean the truth always does get out—even officially. But look how long it takes—look at Cole Porter" ["The Gay Life of a Hollywood Square," OUT/LOOK 2, no. 2 (Fall 1989): 26; this issue is marked as no. 6 on its cover].

3. As quoted in Mary Livingstone Benny, Hilliard Marks, and Marcia Borie, *Jack Benny: A Biography* (Garden City, N.Y.: Doubleday, 1978), 231.

4. Milt Josefsberg, *The Jack Benny Show* (New Rochelle, N.Y.: Arlington House, 1977), 97. One notable exception to Benny's playing the straight man as Jack came when the play *George Washington Slept Here* was adapted to film (1942, Warners, William Keighley) to costar Benny and Ann Sheridan. The play was recast so that Benny took what was originally the wife's role, while Sheridan played the husband's part. "The writers who were adapting the play only had to make a handful of minor changes," Benny recalled. "Otherwise Jean Dixon's speeches were intact but spoken by me, and Miss Sheridan had all [Ernest] Truex's speeches." Jack Benny and Joan Benny, *Sunday Nights at Seven: The Jack Benny Story* (New York: Warner Books, 1990), 146–47.

5. Ibid., 132–33.

6. Arthur Frank Wertheim, *Radio Comedy* (New York: Oxford University Press, 1979), 131.

7. Josefsberg, *Benny Show*, 356.

8. Irving Fein, *Jack Benny: An Intimate Biography* (New York: Putnam, 1976), 24.

9. Benny, Marks, and Borie, *Jack Benny*, 221.

10. Ibid., 250.

11. Ibid., 35, 91.

12. As stated on "The Arsenio Hall Show" (January 2–3, 1990, CBS).

13. Josefsberg, *Benny Show*, 332.

14. *The Jack Benny Program* (November 18, 1945, NBC Blue-Radio Network). All subsequent references to this radio program will be noted in the text by individual program broadcast dates.

15. Josefsberg, *Benny Show*, 351–56.

16. Two moments from the biographies are interesting in this regard. Joan Benny prefaces the section of her father's autobiography on Eddie ("Rochester") Anderson with the following vehement denial of her father's alleged stinginess: "Before we get to Rochester, let me clear up another character—the most important one: Daddy. In real life he wasn't cheap, not even in any way, shape or form! That portrayal was a total myth. It's amazing to me that so many people believed it to be the truth" (p. 97). In a discussion of Mel Blanc's work on *The Jack Benny Program*, Josefsberg recalls, "In one bit we wrote we had Jack ask a man something on a street, and in the stage directions we had written the instructions: 'Mel answers, using the voice of a Colored, Jewish Fag.' Damned if he didn't do it, but it never got on the air" (*Benny Show*, 103).

Benny's name is also invoked in a series of interviews with lesbians about mass culture conducted by Claire (formerly Judy) Whitaker, "Hollywood Transformed: Interviews with Lesbian Viewers," *Jump Cut* 24–25 (1981): 33–35; rpt. in *Jump Cut: Hollywood, Politics, and Counter-Cinema*, ed. Peter Steven (New York: Praeger,

1981), 106–18. When the interviewer asks J. A. Marquis, "How did a Jewish background affect your attitudes about film characters?" she answers, "My parents used to point people out to me and say 'He's Jewish,' as with Jack Benny." Later in the interview, Marquis talks about identifying with women of color in films, such as Lena Horne and Carmen Miranda: "Somehow I always felt a little better when she [Horne] or Carmen Miranda showed up. Somebody who's different, not like all the others." Marquis's pulling together Jewishness, color, and queerness during her interview seems to indicate the workings of a general cultural paradigm also evident in *The Jack Benny Program* (see also note 41 to this chapter).

17. Benny and Benny, *Sunday Nights*, 100.

18. Wertheim, *Radio Comedy*, 140.

19. Benny and Benny, *Sunday Nights*, 111.

20. Ibid.

21. Imamu Amiri Baraka, *Jello* (Chicago: Third World Press, 1970), 9.

22. Fein, *Jack Benny*, 92.

23. Allan Bérubé, *Coming Out under Fire: The History of Gay Men and Women in World War II* (New York: Plume, 1990), 67–97.

24. Josefsberg, *Benny Show*, 86.

25. Ibid., 353.

26. Ibid., 410.

27. In his autobiography, Benny describes Harris and his character on the program in highly sexually charged terms: "He was completely immoral. The character was so written and so played that you knew Phil Harris was probably the finest fornicator of all time. When he made his first speech, which was usually a simple, 'Hiya Jackson,' he somehow got across the idea that he had come to the studio right after having experienced a most satisfying orgasm" (*Sunday Nights*, 118). When combined with the gay innuendo often surrounding Harris's character and his relationship with Jack on the show, Benny's assessment here suggests the possibility Harris's character can be read as bisexual.

28. Fein, *Jack Benny*, 114–15.

29. Ibid., 119–20.

30. Benny and Benny, *Sunday Nights*, 104–5.

31. Ibid., 105.

32. Ibid., 107.

33. Ibid., 130.

34. Joseph Boskin, *Sambo: The Rise and Demise of an American Jester* (New York: Oxford University Press, 1986), 190.

35. Leslie Fiedler, *An End to Innocence: Essays on Culture and Politics* (Boston: Beacon Hill, 1955), 147.

36. Ibid.

37. This interracial gay "mythos" remains an important American cultural fantasy to the present day: see the *Lethal Weapon* films (1987, 1989, 1992; Warners; Richard Donner), *An Officer and a Gentleman* (1982, Paramount, Taylor Hackford), *He's My Girl* (1987, Scott Bros., Gabrielle Beaumont), and the episode of *Roc* (1991–present, Fox) in which the brother of the title character marries a white man, among other examples. For an insightful feminist reading of the interracial erotics of the *Lethal Weapon* films, see the "Lethal Bodies" chapter of Tania Modleski, *Feminism*

without Women: Culture and Criticism in a "Postfeminist" Age (New York and London: Routledge, 1991), 135–63.

38. Richard C. Toll, *Blacking Up: The Minstrel Show in Nineteenth Century America* (New York: Oxford University Press, 1974), 142.

39. Ibid.

40. *Big Boy* (1930, Warners-First National, Alan Crosland). All dialogue is taken from a print of the film.

41. *Big Boy* has an amazing coda, in which Jolson appears on a stage with what we have taken to be the film's cast. Dropping his broad black dialect, Jolson "comes out" as Jewish and white to the theater audience within the film. It appears the film has actually been a stage performance. The layers of deception, passing, and revelation here most insistently involve race and ethnicity, but "the love that dare not speak its name," though connoted throughout the text, remains closeted. Even so, this conjunction of Jewishness, blackness, and gayness, in which race becomes the substitute, visible code for ethnic and sexual difference, links *Big Boy* with *The Jack Benny Program* and any number of other Western mass culture texts.

Western culture's complex associations of queerness (gayness in particular), Jewishness, and blackness deserve a separate study. Two works that begin to explore these connections in relation to cultural texts are Sander L. Gilman's "Strauss, the Pervert, and Avant-Garde Opera of the Fin de Siècle," *New German Critique* 43 (Winter 1988): 35–68; and Michael Rogin's "Blackface, White Noise: The Jewish Jazz Singer Finds His Voice," *Critical Inquiry* 18, no. 3 (Spring 1992): 417–53. Using Richard Strauss's opera of Oscar Wilde's *Salome* as his reference point, Gilman's article traces how late nineteenth- and early twentieth-century discourses of the Jew, the homosexual, the avant-garde, and the feminine were often associated in Western culture. Rogin's piece focuses upon Al Jolson's film *The Jazz Singer* (1927, Warners, Alan Crosland) as part of a critical examination of how Jewish entertainers used blackface earlier in this century. A small section of Rogin's article concerns moments when cross-dressing was added to the spectacle of Jewish performers in blackface, as in Eddie Cantor's drag, blackface stage performance of *Salome*. While these discussions of cross-dressing, blackface, and Jewishness are carried out with reference to straight male Oedipal theoretical models, Rogin suggests a queer approach to this material when he admits that "in relying on hostile accounts of cross-dressing, I am neglecting an important strand in feminist theory" (note 5, pp. 441). He goes on to refer readers to queer-feminist theorist Judith Butler's *Gender Trouble: Feminism and the Subversion of Identity* (New York: Routledge, 1990), among other texts.

42. The frequent domestication of queer interracial erotics also occurs in lesbian mass culture texts, most notably in the two film versions of *Imitation of Life* (1934, Universal, John Stahl; 1959, Universal, Douglas Sirk).

43. "Jack Benny's Man 'Rochester,' " *TV Guide* (August 27, 1955): 20–21.

44. Boskin, *Sambo*, 195.

45. Ibid., 191, 193.

46. Just how complex the characters and relationship of Jack and Rochester became is indicated by the opening of a 1957 episode of the television series. In his role as servant-housewife, Rochester greets a mail carrier at the door, responding to each of the magazines the carrier has brought for Jack. Given *Lonelyhearts* magazine, Rochester looks indifferent and utters a bored "uh huh." *Women's Home Companion* elicits a smile and a sheepish "uh huh," while on being handed *Muscle and Body*

Development, Rochester looks somewhat perturbed and forces out an embarrassed "uh huh." Finally, however, the mail carrier finds a copy of the *Wall Street Journal* for Rochester, who explains that he subscribes to the newspaper because he owns two shares of Jack: "I bought it at thirty-nine. It's been there for ten years!"

47. Ibid., 191.

48. Ibid.

49. Benny and Benny, *Sunday Nights,* 103–4.

50. Gilbert Seldes, *The Public Arts* (New York: Simon and Schuster, 1956), 156–57.

51. Benny and Benny, *Sunday Nights,* 111.

52. Ibid., 113.

5. The Sissy Boy, the Fat Ladies, and the Dykes

1. Bryan Bruce, "Pee Wee Herman: The Homosexual Subtext," *CineAction!* 9 (Summer 1987): 6.

2. Ian Balfour, "The Playhouse of the Signifier: Reading Pee-wee Herman," *Camera Obscura* 17 (1988): 155–56.

3. Ibid., 156.

4. Ibid.

5. I am assuming Paul Reubens is queer, as I do later for Dolly Parton. While having my assumptions validated by public statements might be important to some of my points in this section, such a public disclosure would not significantly alter most of my discussion about Pee-wee and gayness/queerness. In any case, Reubens (like a number of celebrities) is *considered to be* gay, or otherwise queer, by some portion of the queer and straight publics because this is how they read his Pee-wee Herman persona. By rarely appearing out of character, Reubens encouraged the near-erasure of his private life, and the substitution of the public figure of Pee-wee in its place. Therefore, gayness (or a less specific queerness) is part of the range of readings audiences have given Reubens and/as Pee-wee. For an interesting examination of Dolly Parton's place in lesbian culture, see Jean Carlomusto's video *L Is for the Way You Look* (1991). As for Sandra Bernhard and k. d. lang, whom I also mention later in this section, both have more or less come out and come forward about their queer sexuality: Bernhard through remarks about a lover she refers to as "she" in *Madonna: Truth or Dare* (1991, Miramax, Alex Keshishian), and lang in an interview with Brendan Lemon for *The Advocate,* issue 605 (June 16, 1992): 34–46.

6. My use of "sissy" and "sissy boy" to describe preadult feminine queer men is an attempt to capture the position of many homosexual men, like Reubens, who as children were defined and labeled as "sissies" (or "girly") by the straight world. The challenge for these queer men (among whom I count myself) in later years is to work with, through, or around the pejorative straight gender politics that are deployed when a person is labeled "sissy" or "effeminate."

7. Constance Penley, "The Cabinet of Dr. Pee-wee: Consumerism and Sexual Terror," *Camera Obscura* 17 (1988): 147. Program citied: *Pee-wee's Playhouse* (1986-91, CBS).

8. The following sources provide invaluable queer cultural and historical background for working through visual and aural codings of queerness and gender — in life and in representation: Derek Cohen and Richard Dyer, "The Politics of Gay Culture," in *Homosexualities Power and Politics,* ed. Gay Left Collective (London and

New York: Allison and Busby, 1980), 172–86; Christine Riddiough, "Culture and Politics," in *Pink Triangles,* ed. Pam Mitchell (Boston: Alyson, 1980), 14–33; Jackie Goldsby, "What It Means to Be Colored Me," OUT/LOOK 3, no. 1 (Summer 1990): 8–17; Marlon Riggs, "Black Macho Revisited: Reflections of a Snap! Queen," *The Independent* 14, no. 3 (April 1991): 32–34; Marlon Riggs, "Ruminations of a Snap Queen: What Time Is It?" OUT/LOOK 12 (1991): 12–19; Kobena Mercer and Isaac Julien, "Race, Sexual Politics and Black Masculinity: A Dossier," in *Male Order: Unwrapping Masculinity,* ed. Rowena Chapman and Jonathan Rutherford (London: Lawrence and Wishart, 1988), 97–164; Amber Hollinbaugh and Cherrié Moraga, "What We're Rollin Around in Bed With: Sexual Silences in Feminism," in *Powers of Desire: The Politics of Sexuality,* ed. Ann Snitow, Christine Stansell, and Sharon Thompson (New York: Monthly Review Press, 1983), 394–405; Joan Nestle, "The Fem Question," in *Pleasure and Danger: Exploring Female Sexuality,* ed. Carole Vance (London: Pandora Press, 1989), 232–41; Joan Nestle, "Butch-Femme Relationships: Sexual Courage in the 1950s," *A Restricted Country* (Ithaca, N.Y.: Firebrand Books, 1987), 100–109; "Sensibility and Survival," New Gay Arts, A Special Issue, *Village Voice* (June 28, 1988): 21–39; Esther Newton, "Of Yams, Grinders, & Gays," OUT/LOOK 1, no. 1 (Spring 1988): 28–37; Madeline Davis and Elizabeth Lapovsky, "Oral History and the Study of Sexuality in the Lesbian Community: Buffalo, New York, 1940–1960," in *Hidden from History: Reclaiming the Lesbian and Gay Past,* ed. Martin Bauml Duberman, Martha Vicinus, and George Chauncy (New York: New American Library, 1989), 426–40; Sue-Ellen Case, "Toward a Butch-Femme Aesthetic," *Discourse* 11, no. 1 (Fall-Winter 1988–1989): 55–71; Lisa Duggan, "The Anguished Cry of an 80s Fem: I Want To Be a Drag Queen," OUT/LOOK 1, no. 1 (Spring 1988): 62–65; Jan Brown, "Sex, Lies, & Penetration: A Butch Finally 'Fesses Up," OUT/LOOK 2, no. 3 (Winter 1990): 30–34; Arlene Stein, "All Dressed Up, But No Place to Go? Style Wars and the New Lesbianism," OUT/LOOK 1, no. 4 (Winter 1989): 34–44; Mark Leger, "The Boy Look," OUT/LOOK 1, no. 4 (Winter 1989): 45; Julia Creet, "Lesbian Sex/Gay Sex: What's the Difference?" OUT/LOOK 11 (Winter 1991): 29–34; Jan Zita Grover, "The Demise of the Zippered Sweatshirt: Hal Fischer's *Gay Semiotics*," OUT/LOOK 11 (Winter 1991): 44–47; Michelangelo Signorile, "Clone Wars," *Outweek* 74 (November 28, 1990): 39–45; Martin Humphries, "Gay Machismo," in *The Sexuality of Men,* ed. Andy Metcalf and Martin Humphries (London: Pluto Press, 1985), 70–85; Seymour Kleinberg, "Where Have All the Sissies Gone?" in *Alienated Affections* (New York: St. Martin's Press, 1980), 143–56. Besides these specific pieces, many issues of OUT/LOOK, *Outweek, The Advocate, On Our Backs,* and *Bad Attitude* (as well as local and more "underground" lesbian, gay, and bisexual papers and magazines) have articles, columns, photographs, and drawings that touch upon issues of queer style, gender and sexuality attitudes, and media and art representation.

9. Penley, "Dr. Pee-wee," 147.

10. Tania Modleski, "The Incredible Shrinking He[r]man: Male Regression, the Male Body, and Film," *differences* 2, no. 2 (Summer 1990): 64.

11. Modleski, "Shrinking He[r]man," 66.

12. In an editorial comment on this section, Chris Straayer (of the Cinema Studies Department, New York University), wondered if gay misogyny might not be discussed as a form of "gay-straightness"—that is, as instances of gay men expressing attitudes they have taken from the straight male culture around them. This would appear to be

Modleski's point; and perhaps it is the reason she finally conflates straight and gay men in her discussions of misogyny, Pee-wee, camp, and the postmodern. Certainly all—gays, lesbians, straight women, queers—take their original cues from the patriarchy for misogynistic attitudes and expressions. And whether their source is straight or queer, male or female, all expressions of misogyny are reprehensible. But culturally and psychologically, women's, gays', lesbians', and other queer-identified people's misogyny could only be exactly like that of straight men if these former groups' relations to power were the same as that of straight men.

While gay men are "men," I doubt that many can fully ignore or forget that their position in the scheme of straight patriarchal cultures is still a feminized one in the sense that conflates "the feminine" with "woman" and trivializes or reviles the qualities ascribed to the "feminine-woman." Gay men might internalize patriarchal notions of the feminine-woman, or they might accept the conventional characteristics of the feminine-woman while rejecting the pejorative attitudes, or they might attempt to reconceptualize "femininity" (and "masculinity") and its alignment with "woman" (and "man"), or they might reject straight patriarchal conceptions of gender and gender characteristics and formulate alternatives. But no matter which position they take, those gays who in some manner function under the signs of gender must have different understandings of their relation to the concepts of "woman" and "the feminine," and therefore must have cultural and psychological foundations for their misogyny different from those of straight men.

13. Of interest to the ongoing discussions of camp in general and in relation to Pee-wee Herman in particular is "Where Have All the Sissies Gone?," a chapter of Seymour Kleinberg's *Alienated Affections: Being Gay in America* (New York: St. Martin's Press, 1980), 143–56. In part a defense of camp by a feminine gay man (a "sissy"), Kleinberg's comments are compelling reminders that camp critiques referring to queer texts such as *Pee-wee's Playhouse* need to be careful and rigorous about considering queer cultures and queer spectators in their working through the ideological meanings of camp's uses: "Camping did express self-denigration, but it was a complex criticism. . . . Camping also released for gay men some of their anger at their closeted lives. . . . Between the values of virility that they did not question and their rage at having no apparent alternatives, gay men would camp out their frustrations" (pp. 149–50). Implicit in Kleinberg's comments here is the idea that becoming a traditionally feminine straight woman is not, and was not, seen by many "sissies" as the alternative to "virility," that is, to taking on the attributes of straight men. Through camping, sissy gays can create alternatives to those conventional notions of masculinity and femininity that are fused with biologically essentialist conceptions of being a "man" or a "woman." Camping often split culturally constructed gender attributes and labels ("masculinity," "femininity") from the biological categories ("male," "female," "man," "woman") to which straight culture links them. In spite of this queer cultural work, however, straight culture continues by and large to see gay men (whether butch, feminine, or androgynous) as fundamentally "like women" or as "feminine" and treats them accordingly. This straight cultural tenet has an interesting history in the West, some of which is suggested by the title of a lecture given by George Chauncey, Jr., at Cornell University (February 24, 1992): "Why Were Female Prostitutes and Male Homosexuals Linked in the Early Twentieth Century?"

Gay artists and performers might often be seen as reversing the terms of straight culture's "gay men-as-straight women" ideas, by presenting representations of "straight women-as-gay men": think of certain films of R. W. Fassbinder (*Veronika Voss*, 1982; *The Marriage of Maria Braun*, 1978; *Lola*, 1982; *Ali: Fear Eats the Soul*, 1973; *Frauen in New York*, 1977); Pedro Almodóvar (*Women on the Verge of a Nervous Breakdown*, 1988; *High Heels*, 1991; *Tie Me Up! Tie Me Down!*, 1990), George Cukor (*The Women*, 1939; *Girls About Town*, 1931; *Les Girls*, 1957; and *The Chapman Report*, 1962), Edward Albee's play *Who's Afraid of Virginia Woolf?*, Robert Harling's play *Steel Magnolias*, most of Tennessee Williams's plays, drag performances, and Paul Reubens's Pee-wee Herman texts. The painter Paul Cadmus, responding to a comparison of his nude figures to those of Michelangelo's, said: "I do love his forms. His male nudes are wonderful. Both he and Caravaggio are great favorites of mine. In fact, Michelangelo's women often look like males with grapefruits attached" ("Under Fire," Steve Weinstein, *Genre* [April-May 1992]: 75). Critiques of these representational "reversals" as progressive, self-oppressive, misogynistic, or whatever, would need to consider individual texts, their production contexts, and the cultural contexts of text, creator, and potential reader-critics in order to avoid the sort of "one-size-fits-all" cultural politics I address elsewhere in this chapter.

14. Penley, "Dr. Pee-wee," 145.

15. This queer blindness takes its most extreme form in articles such as Rob Winning's "Pee Wee Herman Un-Mascs Our Cultural Myths About Masculinity" (*Journal of American Culture* 11, no. 2 [Summer 1988]: 57–63), which discusses Pee-wee's reconceptualization of masculinity in heterocentrist terms. Aside from noting that Pee-wee's "movements vacillate between those of a frenetic child and an effeminate male" (thus suggesting that homosexuality is an immature form of behavior), Winning's article fully recuperates the character and his texts as examples of a kinder, gentler straight masculinity.

16. Along these lines, one might place various aspects of Pee-wee's world sharply within the range of feminine gay experiences as described by a man quoted in Kleinberg: "We fell for masculinity when we were twelve; there must be something to it because it made us gay. Most of us didn't become gay because we fell in love with sissies; we became sissies because we fell in love with men, usually jocks" (154). With critical irony, Kleinberg follows this quote by saying, "It sounds familiar. And so what if one chooses to make one's life pornographic?" (*Alienated Affections*, 154).

17. Cited in Penley's article ("Dr. Pee-wee"), but worth repeating here, is Bryan Bruce's observation that each "attractive man" on *Pee-wee's Playhouse* "represents a specific gay male icon, prominent fantasy figures in homosexual pornography . . . including the sailor (Captain Carl), the black cowboy (Cowboy Curtis), and the muscular, scantily clad lifeguard (Tito), not to mention the escaped con (Mickey) in *Pee Wee's Big Adventure*" (p. 5).

18. Film cited: *Big Top Pee-wee* (1988, Paramount, Randal Kleiser).

19. Penley, "Dr. Pee-wee," 147.

20. Other specific cultural and psychological contexts would complicate straight-(forward) readings of Pee-wee and the fat women characters in his texts in relation to misogyny. Some of these contexts are suggested in Michael Moon and Eve Kosofsky Sedgwick's dialogue essay "Divinity: A Dossier, A Performance Piece, A Little-Understood Emotion," *Discourse* 13, no. 1 (Fall-Winter 1990–91):

"MICHAEL MOON: It was a deep fear of mine as a twelve-year-old boy putting on pubescent weight that after having been a slender child, I was at puberty freakish and unaccountably developing feminine hips and breasts. . . . One happy aspect of the story of my own and other gay men's formation of our adolescent and adult body-images is that the fat, beaming figure of the diva has never been entirely absent from our *imaginaire* . . . as an alternative body-identity fantasy" (p. 13).

"EVE KOSOFSKY SEDGWICK: John Waters and Divine were a celebrated gay-man-and-diva couple" (p. 15).

"MICHAEL MOON: Divine seems to offer a powerful condensation of some emotional and identity linkages—historically dense ones—between fat women and gay men. Specifically, a certain interface between abjection and defiance . . . [which] seems to be related to the interlocking histories of stigma, self-constitution, and epistemological complication proper to fat women and gay men in this century" (p. 15).

"EVE KOSOFSKY SEDGWICK: It follows from all this, however, that there *is* such a process as *coming out as a fat woman.* Like the other, more materially dangerous kind of coming out, it involves a risk—here, a certainty—of uttering bathetically as a brave declaration that truth which can scarcely in this instance ever have been less than self-evident. Also, like the other kind of coming out, however, denomination of oneself as a fat woman is a way in the first place of making clear to others that their cultural meanings will be, and will be heard as, assaultive and diminishing to the degree that they are not fat-affirmative. In the second place and far more importantly, it is a way of staking one's claim to insist on, and participate actively in, a renegotiation of the *representational contract* between one's body and one's world" (p. 27).

Throughout this dialogue, Moon's and Sedgwick's comments about the often symbiotic relationships of (feminine) gay men and fat women—which are pitched somewhere between "abjection and defiance"—suggest a number of provocative approaches to queerly reading Reubens's construction of, and Pee-wee's interactions with, Mrs. Steve, Mrs. Rene, the Cowntess, and even the voluptuous Miss Yvonne, as something other than examples of misogyny.

21. The works referred to here are *The Women* (1939, MGM, George Cukor), and *Frauen in New York* (1977, Ndr Television, R. W. Fassbinder).

22. Works cited: *Pee-wee's Big Adventure* (1985, Paramount, Tim Burton), *The Pee-wee Herman Show* (1981, HBO, Marty Callner).

23. Modleski, "Shrinking He[r]man," 63.

24. Ibid., 63–64.

25. Balfour, "Playhouse of the Signifier," 158.

26. Ibid., 156, 166 (note 1).

27. Program cited: *Pee-wee's Playhouse Christmas Special* (1989, CBS, W. Orr and P. Reubens).

28. Given Bernhard's moves between suggesting that men, then women, are the objects of her sexual interest—including her playfully irritating "girlfriend" posing with Madonna and her *Playboy* nude photo layout (39, no. 9, September 1992: 70–77) in which she poses with men and women—Bernhard's public persona might be seen as bisexual rather than as femme dyke. Pee-wee's discomfort with Bernhard's flirtations in the scene cited here, then, might be read as the response of a gay confronted with bisexuality.

29. D. A. Miller, "Anal *Rope,*" *Representations* 32 (Fall 1990): 118–19.

30. Among these sorts of articles and interviews published at the height of the Pee-wee craze were Ian Penman, "America's Sweetheart," *The Face* 87 (July 1987): 14–19, 75; Barry Walters, "Triumph of the Twerp," *Village Voice* (September 23, 1986): 43–44; Jack Barth, "Pee Wee TV," *Film Comment* 22, no. 6 (November-De-

cember 1986): 79; T. Gertler, "The Pee-Wee Perplex," *Rolling Stone* (February 12, 1987): 37–40, 100, 102–3; Margy Rochlin, "Pee-wee Herman," *Interview* 17, no. 7 (July 1987): 45–50.

31. Henry Jenkins III, " 'Going Bonkers!': Children, Play and Pee-wee," *Camera Obscura* 17 (1988): 182.

32. The Penley article does an excellent job of critically analyzing the production history of *Pee-wee's Playhouse*, making a good case for the conscious risks the network took in "transforming a sexually risque work of performance art [*The Pee-wee Herman Show*] into a children's television program." Penley goes on to say that "what is surprising is that CBS never questioned or censored the show's presentation of sexuality, including its clear allusions to homosexuality" ("Dr. Pee-wee," 144–45).

33. Ibid., 136.

34. My gay reading of the sexual connotations surrounding Pee-wee's bicycle is in part a response to Winning's interpretation of the bike in conventional pop Freud dream-fantasy terms as "a potent phallic symbol" because it is "something which is fast, red, has a head, and most importantly, fits between his [Pee-wee's] legs" ("Pee Wee Herman Un-Mascs," 58). In the context of Winning's straight reading of Pee-wee's character, this makes sense, as does seeing the loss of the bike as representing castration anxiety. But I'd like to offer a queer—specifically a gay male—reading of this same bicycle and its symbolic sexual functions in Pee-wee's world. As much as something that "fits between his legs," the bike is something Pee-wee sits on. In his Tour de France dream, Pee-wee "is riding erect," as Winning notes, as he excitedly pedals his bike over the finish line. Rather than Pee-wee's own lost penis or phallus, the bike could represent that of another man. So Pee-wee's activities on his bike would not only represent masturbatory autoeroticism and castration, as the sexual pleasure and loss here could be connected to anal sex or dildo play and the loss of a sex partner or a sex toy.

35. Miller, "Anal *Rope*," 119.

36. At the end of his article, Balfour reminds readers that "the classical sphinx proposed a riddle, a question whose answer, as only Oedipus knew, was 'man' " ("Playhouse of the Signifier," 166). While Balfour suggests that "man" is the question, not the answer, in *Pee-wee's Playhouse*, I would queerly propose that "man" is indeed the answer (as in "I want/need a man"), considering queeny Jambi is the sphinx and gay Pee-wee is our Oedipus. Perhaps a gay version of the Oedipus myth is being suggested here?

Afterword: "You Flush It, I Flaunt It!"

1. Films cited: *Batman Returns* (1992, Warners, Tim Burton), *Buffy the Vampire Slayer* (1992, Twentieth Century-Fox, Fran Rubel Kuzui).

2. For examples of supportive critical pieces written in the wake of Reubens's arrest see: Laurie Stone, "Pee-wee Agonistes," *Village Voice* 36, no. 33 (August 13, 1991): 39; Michael Bronski, "Reel Politick," *Z Magazine* 4, no. 9 (September 1991): 64–67; Fuchs, "Fuchs on Film," *Labyrinth* (a Philadelphia women's newspaper) 8, no. 9 (October 1991): 9; Peter Wilkinson, "Who Killed Pee-wee," *Rolling Stone* 614 (October 3, 1991): 36–38, 41–42, 140.

3. Stone, "Pee-wee Agonistes," 39.

4. Reubens himself was the object of media "inning" after his arrest when tabloids spread stories about him being romantically involved with actress Carol Kane.

These heterosexualizing stories were among the few mass-media reports to allow a note of sympathy for Reubens. For examples see Jerome George and Angela Aiello, "The New Odd Couple," *National Enquirer* (October 8, 1991): 3; "Pee-wee Finds Love with Kooky Kewpie Doll," *Star* (October 8, 1991): 36–37.

5. Works cited (which have not been previously cited): Douglas Crimp, ed., *AIDS: Cultural Analysis/Cultural Activism* (Cambridge, Mass.: MIT Press, 1989); Robin Wood, *Hollywood from Vietnam to Reagan* (New York: Columbia University Press, 1986); *The Silence of the Lambs* (1991, Orion, Jonathan Demme); *Basic Instinct* (1992, Tri-Star, Paul Verhoeven); *Tongues Untied* (1990, Marlon Riggs); *Looking for Langston* (1989, Sankofa Film and Video, Isaac Julien); *Out on Tuesdays* (1989–90, Channel 4); *Video Against AIDS* (1990, V. Tape/Canada abd Video Data Bank).

6. Works cited: *In Living Color* (1990–present, Fox); *Lethal Weapon* (1987, Warners, Richard Donner); *Lethal Weapon 2* (1989, Warners, Richard Donner); *Lethal Weapon 3* (1992, Warners, Richard Donner); *Fried Green Tomatoes* (1991, Universal, Jon Avnet); *Bosom Buddies* (1980–82, ABC); *Major Dad* (1989-present, CBS).

7. Works cited: *thirtysomething* (1987–91, ABC); *Heartbeat* (1988–89, ABC); *L.A. Law* (1986–present, NBC); *Northern Exposure* (1990–present, CBS); *Longtime Companion* (1990, Samuel Goldwyn, Norman Rene); *Maurice* (1987, Merchant-Ivory, James Ivory); *The Lost Language of Cranes* (1992, BBC-TV/PBS, Norman Rene).

8. In making this sort of statement, I am disagreeing to some extent with Frankfurt School mass culture critics and with certain British cultural studies theorists, who find that oppositional (sub)cultural styles, attitudes, production, and other mass cultural work can only exert limited or temporary influences within culture at large ("mainstream," "dominant," or "capitalist" culture). Further, these commentators consider that the intersections of (sub)cultures and "mainstream" culture constitute sites at which the latter begins the inevitable process of co-opting, containing, and politically neutralizing the work of (sub)cultures.

While this situation might be the case for other (sub)cultures (and I'm not certain that it is), I think queerness is always already too much a part of "mainstream" culture for it to ever become fully co-opted or contained, particularly within volatile mass culture contexts. If anything, the queerness of and in mass culture—once it has been made visible and vocal—is very difficult to easily assimilate because it is so pervasive and so multifaceted. Although one might point to camp as an example of a queer (mass) culture style or attitude that appears to have been co-opted by nonqueer culture, the "co-optation" here seems to have resulted less in the erasure of queerness than in nonqueer culture recognizing (if not always admitting) that certain aspects of "their" mass culture production, texts, and reception are "camp" and therefore queer or, more specifically, gay. In this way, camp remains connected to queerness, and through the increasing understanding of certain discourses within the mainstream as "camp," queerness is (or might become) recognized as being part of what have been considered nonqueer cultural production, texts, and readers. This mainstream recognition and use of camp has happened alongside more frequent feminist and lesbian uses of camp in relation to mass culture production, reception, and theory. With regards to camp, then, queerness seems to prosper rather than to be contained. So where or what *is* the "mainstream" here?

In terms of understanding mass culture it continues to be important for us to review and reconceptualize traditional notions of "mainstream" and "marginal" texts, cultural influences, and interpretations. Queers, women, African-Americans, Hispanics, the working class, and many other "marginal" groups need to loudly (re)claim their contributions to the "mainstream." The traditional ways we are taught to understand and interpret mass culture as (of course) fundamentally for and about white, male, straight, and middle-class people is both inaccurate and oppressive as it continually reinscribes straight, white patriarchy as the center of—and the point of reference for—all mass culture production and consumption-reception. And we know this just isn't true.

Recently, a youth-culture cousin of camp has sprung up, called "cheese." In a *New York Times* article, "First There Was Camp, Now There's Cheese" (August 7, 1992, C1, C19), Michiko Kakutani compares camp to cheese in a number of important ways, yet finally distinguishes between the two by saying, "Camp tends to be inclusive and generous, whereas Cheese tends to be judgmental, cynical and detached" in its critical send-up of mass culture. In spite of what Kakutani sees as its different attitude toward mass culture, however, it is clear that there would be no cheese if camp was not already so much a part of mainstream culture.

For an interesting overview of how influential gay and lesbian cultures have become in mass culture over the last decade or so, see Barry Walters, "Gay Culture: The Underground Influence Sinks Deep Roots," *Au Courant* 7:37 (July 31, 1989): 1, 7, 9. This article originally appeared during June 1989 as part of the *San Francisco Examiner*'s "Gay in America" series.

Index

ALEXANDER DOTY is currently an associate professor of film, mass culture, and gay and lesbian studies in Lehigh University's English Department. He has published articles in *Camera Obscura, Cinema Journal, Wide Angle, Quarterly Journal of Film and Video,* and in the anthology *Film Comedy in History: Narrative, Performance, Ideology* (AFI/Routledge). An anthology he is editing with Corey Creekmur, *Out in Culture: Lesbian, Gay, and Queer Essays on Film and Mass Culture,* is forthcoming from Duke University Press.